NATIONAL
GEOGRAPHIC
KiDS

POUNCE!

A HOW TO SPEAK CAT TRAINING GUIDE

TRACEY WEST &

GARY WEITZMAN, D.V.M.,

PRESIDENT & CEO OF THE SAN DIEGO HUMANE SOCIETY

NATIONAL GEOGRAPHIC
WASHINGTON, D.C.

CONTENTS

DISCLAIMER: Various steps in some of the activities in this book involve a potential risk of personal injury, property damages, and other dangers. Some potential dangers include cuts and abrasions. By performing and/or allowing your child to perform any activities presented in this book, you (i) assume all risks of damages or injury to any person or property as a result of you and/or your young cat trainer's performance of the activities, and (ii) acknowledge that author and publisher disclaim all responsibility and liability for any damage or injury that may result from you and/or your young cat trainer's performance of the activities.

Meet Dr. Gary

Veterinarian and Cat Expert

Do cats rule the world? Lots of people seem to think so. Many cat owners claim that their feline friends are in control. I've often heard, "My cat is in charge, and there's nothing I can do about it." But I believe that with patience and persistence, all cats can be trained.

My name is Dr. Gary Weitzman, and I'm going to be your guide throughout this book. I've been a veterinarian and an animal rescuer for more than 30 years. I'm currently the president and CEO of the San Diego Humane Society in California, U.S.A. I spend a lot of time making sure that animals are well cared for, have homes, and receive medical care and attention.

A few years ago, two cats named Sky and Abner lived at my veterinary practice. I inherited them from the retired vet who had previously owned the office. They walked around like they owned the place. Everyone was in love with these two felines, so I couldn't take them home.

Sky and Abner would not have been able to live at the veterinary office without training. They had to learn basic things like how to use a litter box. These two also had to be trained to behave in the office. In this book, I'll share strategies for teaching basic skills as well as correcting unwanted behaviors. You'll learn intermediate tricks such as walking your kitty on a leash. And with practice, you can try the advanced tricks, like teaching your cat to jump through a hoop!

At the San Diego Humane Society, we have a nursery dedicated to saving the lives of orphaned kittens from all over our region. We provide them with lots of love and care. We also start all our kittens off with basic training, which includes learning how to interact well with others. You, too, will want to start at the beginning. No matter what your pet's age, make sure to first offer love and care, then let the training begin. Start with the basics first, though. Jumping ahead to the advanced tricks could stress out your cat.

Let's pounce into these pages. You might be surprised at all the wonderful things that you and your feline can do together.

FOR YOUR **SAFETY**

We have made sure that the training tips, scenarios, and interpretations of cat behavior in this book come from the most accurate and up-to-date sources. That said, remember that cats, like all animals, can be unpredictable.

Much of the advice and guidance in this book requires close observation of cats, but even so there may be behavior that the observer (you!) can miss. That means we always need to be cautious with cats—those that are strangers to you and your own pets.

If you are following the steps from this book and your cat seems upset, stop what you are doing and approach it a new way, or try again later.

A NOTE TO **PARENTS**

The activities in this book are designed to be fun for both kids and their pets. Just like humans, cats enjoy new challenges! For safety purposes, we recommend that your young cat trainer have adult supervision for ALL of the activities in this book.

Before your child begins an activity, please read and discuss the following cat SAFETY GUIDELINES with your child, to make sure that both your child and any participating cat are safe, comfortable, and having fun:

CAT SAFETY
- Remember that cats, like all animals, can be unpredictable.
- Only do these activities with your own cat. He should be very comfortable around your child.
- Watch for signs that your cat is unhappy. If any of these activities seem to make your cat uncomfortable or upset, stop immediately.
- Give your cat a break. Make sure he has access to water and if he wants to stop, let him.
- If your cat is on a special diet, check with his veterinarian before feeding him treats. Always check with the cat's owner before feeding him anything.
- Clean up when you are done, so your cat doesn't accidentally eat any leftover materials.
- If you decide to alter an activity or try a new version, make sure the new plan is safe for both your child and the cat.

You Can't **TRAIN** a Cat, Can You?

Yes, you *can* train a cat! Many people think that cats are too independent to be trained. This mistaken belief is common for a few reasons.

Let's start by talking about dogs. Everybody knows that you can train a dog, right? That's because more than 20,000 years ago, when humans first domesticated dogs, they taught them specific jobs. Some dogs were trained to hunt. Others were trained to herd cattle, find lost people, bark out warnings, or do other jobs.

Cats and humans have a shorter history together. About 8,000 years ago, cats began to hang around human settlements. They ate the rodents that were gobbling up the humans' grain supply. Humans saw that cats were useful and kept them around. But we never had to train the cats to eat mice—they did it on their own. So it's true that we never had to train cats in the past, but that doesn't mean that they can't be trained now.

The key to training a cat is finding out what motivates it, and that can be tricky. Why? Most dogs respond to praise, while many cats don't. If you pat your dog on the head and say "Good dog!" he may wag his tail and repeat the good behavior next time. But if you pat your kitty on the head and say "Good cat!" she may not care. Cats can respond to other rewards, too, so don't worry! Once you figure out what reward your cat likes, you'll unlock the key to training your pet.

A cat born with an extra toe is called a polydactyl cat.

Why **TRAIN** Your Cat?

Teaching your cat to ring a bell on command would definitely impress your friends and family. But astounding others with cool tricks is just one of the reasons to train a cat.

A trained cat is a safe cat. If you can teach your cat to get into a carrier, that means you'll be able to take her to the vet easily or keep her from escaping outside if workers or guests are coming over. Training a cat to walk on a leash, instead of letting her go outside on her own, can protect her from dangers such as accidents and disease. If you teach your cat to sit on cue, you'll have an easier time brushing her teeth, which will keep her healthy.

A trained cat is also a happy cat. "Bad" behavior, such as scratching up furniture, could make you and your family upset with your pet. We want you to enjoy living with your pet. It's important to know that you can train a cat to stop unwanted behavior. It will take time and patience, but it will be worth it.

When a cat knows what is expected in a home, she'll fit in better with your human and animal family. You won't get stressed out by your cat's behavior, and your cat won't get stressed when you are upset or when she does something wrong. It's a win for both of you!

Finally, training will help you form a bond with your cat. You'll spend time together and learn how to communicate with each other. You'll learn how to trust and respect each other, too. When your cat is curled up in your lap and purring, you'll be glad you spent the time to make that bond.

A trained cat is a **happy** cat.

BACK

Like other animals with backbones, cats have cushion-like disks between the small bones in their spine. But **their disks are elastic and stretchy.** These, along with their back muscles, allow cats to curve their back in that classic "Halloween cat" pose.

TAIL

The main purpose of a cat's tail is **to help it balance.** If a cat falls from someplace high, the tail helps the cat flip its body around so it lands feetfirst. Cats also use their tails to communicate to humans and other animals.

FUR

Tiny muscles attached to the follicles of a cat's hair allow the cat to make its **fur stand straight up—or bristle.** Combined with an arched back and a hiss, this helps a cat scare off enemies.

LEGS

When a cat walks, it moves the front and back leg **on one side of its body,** and then the front and back leg on the other side. Only a few other animals, such as camels and giraffes, move the same way.

CLAWS

Cats have the ability to retract their claws—pull them up and out of the way—when they're not using them. When cats walk, **they retract their claws so they don't get stuck.**

UNDERSTANDING
Your Cat

Can you speak cat? When you understand how your feline communicates, listens, learns, and explores the world, you can better train your cat.

EARS

Human ears contain five muscles. A cat's ears contain 32, which means that a cat can **turn its ears quickly** in the direction of a sound—even faster than a dog can.

EYES

Cats can see well at night. An extra layer on the back of the cat's eyeball, called the tapetum lucidum, helps the cat see in the darkness. It's also what makes the cat's eyes appear to **glow at night** when the cat's pupils are open. Any light that hits the tapetum bounces back out, making the eyes seem to shine from within.

WHISKERS

A cat's whiskers are very **sensitive to vibrations** and might help the cat sense its environment. The position of a cat's whiskers can also give clues to the cat's mood.

TONGUE

If you've ever been licked by a cat, you know that its tongue **feels like sandpaper.** That is because it is covered in backward-pointing spines, which look like hooks and help a cat groom itself.

Can You **TEACH** an Old Cat New Tricks?

 Kittens are a lot like young children. Place a toddler in any room, and he'll start exploring his environment. He'll run or crawl around and touch things, including items he's not supposed to handle.

Kittens are just as curious and will try to investigate their surroundings. They're also eager to learn new things, so this is a great time to train them. You can teach kittens good behaviors before they have a chance to learn unwanted ones.

But don't worry, you can train an older cat, too! Most cats are able to learn at any age. With an older cat, you might have to spend some time undoing their old habits before they can learn new, better ones. It may take a little extra effort and patience, but the results will be worth it!

DR. GARY'S **TRAINING TIPS**

Between the ages of two and seven weeks, kittens learn to socialize from their mother, their brothers and sisters, and the humans who take care of them. Socialization, or learning to interact with others, is an important time in a kitten's life. In the Kitten Nursery at the San Diego Humane Society, we start socializing them with people from the first week of their lives. After eight weeks, kittens can't learn new ways of socializing. But even feral, or wild, kittens can be socialized if we start early enough!

When kittens are eight weeks old, they are no longer dependent on their mothers and can be adopted. We offer training at our Kitten Kindergarten for kittens ages eight to 16 weeks to reinforce what they've already learned, and to build on it. This is when they are most receptive to learning something new.

In class, kittens are exposed to new people, places, smells, sights, and sounds. They get used to being handled by humans, which is important at this stage of life. After this training, they are more likely to mature into friendly and social adult cats.

Every cat has a **different pattern** of tiny ridges and bumps on the skin of his nose. This "noseprint" is as unique as a **human fingerprint.**

Training and Care for ALL AGES

Maybe you're reading this book because you have a brand-new kitten, and you want to start off on the right paw. Maybe you've never tried training your cat, and you want to see what she can learn. Or you may have an older cat that needs some training to fix an unwanted habit. You should approach training differently depending on the age of your feline friend.

Kittens and Young Cats (0–2 Years)

While kittens are usually easier to train than older cats, they have much shorter attention spans. That means you should keep kitten-training sessions brief, from five to 10 minutes. Focus these sessions on only one skill.

When you become a kitten owner, the first thing you and your family need to do is bring your pet to a vet. A vet will check your kitten to make sure she's healthy and will talk to you about vaccinations your cat will need to protect her from diseases.

The Safety Circle activity on page 31 is especially important for kittens!

Adult Cats (3–10 Years)

As cats get older, they can gain excess weight, so play and training are excellent ways to help your cat exercise. Adult cats are in their prime hunting years. You can tap into those hunting instincts to get them to play. Motorized toys that they can chase around are great for this.

Some adult cats may have learned unwanted behaviors, so part of your training will be to help them unlearn those behaviors.

The Shell Game on page 156 is a fun way to tap into your adult cat's hunting instincts.

Older Cats (11 Years and Older)

Once cats reach age 11, they become less active. They sleep more, and they might not want to play as much. Before you begin a training session with an older cat, make sure you pay attention to her body language (page 24). If she's not interested, put off training for another time.

Older cats can develop medical problems that might affect their training. Some develop arthritis, a disease that harms their joints. You should avoid jumping tricks if your cat is arthritic. It's always good to check with your vet about what your cat can comfortably do.

To make life more pleasant for your older cat, provide soft, cozy, quiet places for her to sleep. Older cats like things warmer, too.

If you're worried about physically stressing your older cat, try an activity like Walk on a Leash on page 82. But keep your walks short!

Cat Stats QUIZ

HOW MUCH DO YOU KNOW ABOUT CATS? Grab a sheet of paper and write down the numbers 1 through 10. Then write down whether you think the statements below are true or false. Check your answers at the bottom of the page to see how many feline facts you got right!

1. Cats purr only when they are happy.
2. Cats claw furniture because it is a natural behavior.
3. Cats are vegetarian.
4. Black cats are bad luck.
5. The average household cat weighs 6 to 10 pounds (2.7 to 4.5 kg).
6. A cat's mouth can help it smell things.
7. More U.S. households have dogs than they do cats.
8. Cats cannot swim.
9. Cats have nine lives.
10. A town in Alaska, U.S.A., once had a cat for a mayor.

1. False. They also purr when they are hurt, so scientists think purring might be a way that cats calm themselves. 2. True. Wild cats such as lions claw trees. Scientists think they do it to sharpen their claws, or just to stretch. 3. False. 4. False. This misconception has led to the cruel treatment of black cats. 5. True. 6. True. An organ that helps them process smells is located in the roof of a cat's mouth. 7. True, but there are more pet cats in the United States than dogs because cat owners tend to own multiple cats. 8. False. They don't like water, but they are natural swimmers. 9. False. Cats only live once, but they are often able to survive falls from high places, which is where this legend comes from. 10. True. Stubbs the cat was honorary mayor of Talkeetna, Alaska, for 10 years.

BEFORE YOU BEGIN

THIS MAY BE the most important chapter in the book, so don't skip it! It's tempting to jump ahead to the cool tricks in later chapters. But there are some good reasons why you shouldn't. For one, you might stress or even harm your cat. Also, you probably won't be successful. Why? Many of these tricks build on one another and your cat needs to master some tricks before he can advance.

You need to learn some things, too—like what makes your cat tick. In this chapter you'll learn about cat body language and behavior. This will help you recognize cues so you know when your cat is ready to learn or when you are better off waiting until your pet is in a more approachable mood.

Training a cat requires some simple and inexpensive equipment. This chapter will help you become familiar with all these tools and show you the skills needed to use them. We'll even show you how to practice the training steps with your human friends first, so you'll have a better understanding of what your cat will experience. Ask an adult to supervise and then let's go!

TOOLS TO GET STARTED

Most of the activities and tricks in this chapter require a few simple items:

▶ A cat training clicker (see page 34)

▶ A target stick (see page 40)

▶ Cat treats (see page 35)

▶ Cat toys (see page 146)

Personalize Your
TRAINING

If you like cats, then you already understand that no two are alike. Some of them run up to greet visitors, while others run and hide. Some cats love to cuddle, while others will make you earn their affection. And some cats look forward to training with their owners, while others can be reluctant.

The simple fact is that some cats can be trained more easily than others. That doesn't mean you shouldn't try to train a shy or an unruly cat. But it does mean that you need to pay attention to your pet's mood before and during a training session. And always, remember:

- Always train with your own cat and ask an adult to supervise.
- Don't force your cat to do something. If she seems angry or stressed, stop what you're doing, leave her, and try again another time.
- Never yell at your cat. As you're about to learn, positive reinforcement is the best way to train an animal. That means you'll need to give her praise. But most of all, be patient!
- Never hit your cat. Even a simple swat could frighten her or stress her out. A stressed-out cat is not able to learn, and this will definitely hurt the bond you are trying to create!
- When in doubt, ask a vet! Regular healthy visits to the vet are important. Anytime you are concerned, don't hesitate to ask your vet. Your vet will want to make sure there is nothing physically wrong with your cat that is making her resistant to training or causing unwanted behaviors. Some vets are even experts in animal behavior!

DR. GARY'S **TRAINING TIPS**

Pay attention to how your cat is acting. Is your cat trying to move away from you, or shutting down and not paying attention to you? That's a sign that this isn't a good time to train.

Reading Your Cat's **BODY LANGUAGE**

Before you begin any training with your cat, take a look at his body language. He can't speak in words, but he can tell you a lot with his face, his tail, and the way he holds his body. Keep an eye out for these signals while you're training, too. If you see one of these, it's time to stop the training session.

⤵ FLATTENED EARS

A cat with ears flattened on top of his head might be telling you he's scared—or that he's ready for a fight.

⤵ EARS TURNED SIDEWAYS

Normally, the opening to your cat's ears face front. If they rotate to face backward or to the side, it probably means your cat is angry.

↩ WHISKERS POINTING BACKWARD

If your cat's whiskers are flattened against his face, he's likely feeling scared or even aggressive.

⟨⇄ TWITCHING TAIL

Back and forth, back and forth ... if your cat is moving his tail like this, he might be feeling uneasy or annoyed.

⟨⟩ HUNKERED DOWN

If your cat is lying on his belly with his shoulders hunched and head down, it's a sign of anxiety or even fear.

⟨⇄ BACK ARCHED

A cat with an arched back, like the kind you see in Halloween decorations, is afraid and trying to tell you to stay away.

I WANT TO **PLAY**

Your cat's body language can also tell you when he's in the mood to play or interact. If he rolls over on his back or stands up and holds out his front paws, those are probably signs that he's in a happy mood. But don't rub his belly. Cats, unlike dogs, don't like that very much!

Some researchers think that when **house cats** make a **chattering sound,** they might be trying to **mimic nearby birds.**

UNDERSTANDING
Natural Behaviors

Cats were wild animals until about 8,000 years ago, when they first started hanging out with humans. After cats became domesticated, meaning they were tamed and kept as pets, those wild behaviors continued. Even if your cat has never been outside, these natural behaviors are likely to show up in the way he acts in your home and interacts with you.

Cats Are Hunters
In the wild, cats eat small animals. Mother cats teach their kittens to catch prey, release it, and catch it again. They have to do this to learn how to best capture their prey. When your cat plays with you, he is re-creating the playtime he had with his mom and acting out his predator training. But don't worry—he's just having fun with you!

Cats Are Afraid of Danger
While cats might be predators, in the wild they face danger from larger animals and even other cats. To stay safe, they'll hide wherever they can such as the hollow of a tree. In your house, they might climb into an empty cardboard box. From there, they can observe their surroundings without being seen, and it makes them feel safe.

Cats Mark Their Territory
In the wild, cats scratch on trees to leave behind their scent so that other cats know to stay away. Without trees (or cat trees!), your cat might scratch the furniture instead.

Cats Pounce
A cat on the hunt may hide and wait patiently for a bird or a mouse to walk by—and then he will pounce! When your cat jumps on a falling leaf or at a shadow, he is acting out this behavior.

Understanding your cat's natural behaviors is the first step in training. Once you understand why your cat acts a certain way, it's easier to train him to stop.

PRE-TRAINING Test

 This simple test will allow you to figure out how your cat reacts to new and unfamiliar things. First, read over this page, and then get an adult's permission before you begin.

Next, choose a room where your cat spends a lot of time. The room will need to have a door so you can keep your pet enclosed in the space. Go into the room with your cat. Hang out and let her explore. After five minutes, remove your cat from the room while you prepare the test.

When you return alone to the room, change one or more things in it. For example, you could move a table from one side to the other, put your backpack in the center of the floor, or take away a favorite chair. You don't have to rearrange the whole room, but make sure the changes you make are different enough that your cat will notice.

Now bring your cat back into the room and close the door. Stay with her and watch her. How does she react to the changes in the room? Does she walk around calmly, curiously checking out the changes? Or does she seem frightened? Does she try to leave?

If your cat is calm and curious, that means she is an excellent cat for training. Wait! That doesn't mean that you can jump to the advanced tricks in the book, but it means she is likely to be attentive and interested during training sessions.

If your cat is afraid, then you need to be extra patient and cautious when introducing her to new things. You may need to proceed a little more slowly. It doesn't mean that she can't be trained—only that you need to be persistent and patient in order for her to succeed.

DR. GARY'S VET TIPS

Your cat might start out as a shy cat, but that doesn't mean she will always be shy. At the San Diego Humane Society, we have transformed thousands of shy cats into confident cats, and training is the best way to do that. On the flip side, if you've got a high-energy cat, training that includes a lot of play can help your cat release that extra energy and calm down.

SAFETY CIRCLE
for Kittens

Have you recently brought home a new kitten? For the first two to four weeks she is in her new home, introduce her to playtime! Before you start clicker training (more on that later), you will need to spend some time interacting with her in a safety circle. If you're training an older cat, you can skip this step.

A safety circle is any designated space in the shape of a circle that is safe for your four-legged friend. The circle should be free of furniture, cords, electrical outlets, or anything else that might harm a curious kitten. A playpen works great, but you don't need to buy one. You can make a safety circle using pillows or rolled-up towels.

Put some kitten-safe toys inside the circle you've created. The best toys for tiny kittens are small balls or plush toys with no removable parts. Only use toys specifically designed for cats. Avoid yarn, ribbon, and feather toys, which could cause a kitten to choke. Do not use toys with large holes that kittens could get stuck in. When in doubt, ask your pet shop for advice. And be sure to read the label on any store-bought goods so you use them properly.

Once you place your kitten inside the safety circle, let her have fun! Use the toys to encourage your kitten to play and explore in the circle. Lightly roll a ball or move a plush toy around the circle. This will help you bond with your pet. Since it is a play session and not a training session, it can be longer than 10 minutes. But don't go on for too long, or your kitten may get tired.

Remember to set up the circle in a quiet room with no distractions. If your kitten appears agitated or upset, stop the play session immediately and try again at another time.

DR. GARY'S **TRAINING TIPS**

Most behaviors are set in stone for cats by the time they are eight weeks old. After eight weeks, their brains sort of lock in to the behavior they've learned. Even feral, or wild, kittens can be socialized if we start them before eight weeks of age. When a kitten is two weeks old, you can begin to socialize her with humans and other animals. Between eight and 16 weeks of age, those socialization skills can be reinforced.

TRAINING Tips

In order to get started on the right paw, follow these guidelines when you begin to train your cat:

Train in a Quiet Place

Choose a place with no distractions for your training session. That means no music playing, no TV blaring, no appliances going, and no other people or animals making noise. You want your cat to be focused on you and only you!

Set a Time

If you can, train at the same time every day. That will get your cat used to the routine, and she may even look forward to your training sessions. If possible, choose a time of day when your cat is hungry (not right after a meal) so she will be more interested in your treats as rewards.

Keep It Short

A 10-minute session is the perfect length for cat training, and in the beginning your sessions will probably be even shorter. Your cat may become more patient as you progress, but it's OK if your early sessions last for just a few minutes. Remember, no matter how long you've been going, stop as soon as your cat acts impatient or irritable.

On average, **cats sleep 16 hours** a day.

CLICKER
Training Tools

For cat training, we recommend using a small device called a clicker, along with treats or some other kind of reward. Most of the tricks in this book require a clicker and treats.

Why use a clicker? When you speak to a cat, your voice might change its tone. Your cat might be unsure how to respond to these different tones and wonder whether each change in your voice means something different. The clicker device always makes the same sound: a loud click. In training, your cat will learn that when he hears that click, he will get a reward. And with that encouragement, your cat will have the necessary motivation to learn commands and tricks.

Even though you're using a clicker, it's fine to shower your cat with praise at the end of a training session. That will help strengthen the bond between you and your pet.

IF YOUR CAT IS DEAF, try using a penlight instead of a clicker. Flash the penlight on and off quickly instead of using a clicker during the training session.

DR. GARY'S **VET TIPS**

Using a clicker is easy. Simply press the button on it, and it will make a clicking sound. In this book, when you see the word "click," it means press the button on the clicker.

TREATS!

The best treats to use when training are whatever your cat prefers. Because all cats are different, you'll need to figure out what he likes best. (Try doing the treat test on page 148.) It's important to make sure whatever you feed your cat is healthy and safe. Check with an adult before you give your cat any food. Here are Dr. Gary's recommendations:

BEST TREATS

- Small pieces of cooked tuna fish, turkey, or chicken
- Bonito flakes (Japanese dried fish)
- Tiny treats you can find in the supermarket (be sure that they don't have a lot of artificial ingredients)
- Dental treats you can find at a pet store, which may help clean your cat's teeth

UNSAFE TREATS AND OTHER FOODS

- Bacon, which is too fatty and could harm your cat's health over time
- Cheese and milk are hard for some cats to digest, so avoid them
- Grapes and raisins are highly poisonous to cats
- Xylitol, a sugar substitute, can cause low blood sugar and liver damage
- Coffee
- Chocolate
- Energy drinks
- Onions
- Garlic
- Raw eggs

64-Square
CLICKER PRACTICE

Before you use the clicker with your cat, practice using it with friends or family members first. This game will give you an idea of how the clicker works and may even give you a hint about how your cat will feel during training.

YOU NEED
- Paper and pencil
- Chalk or masking tape
- One or more friends
- A clicker
- A stopwatch or a phone with a timer

INSTRUCTIONS

1. Draw an eight-by-eight grid of squares on the paper. Then draw a path through the grid, like a maze that starts and ends on outside squares. Don't show your friends!

2. Create another eight-by-eight grid of squares outside using chalk. Make the squares big enough for a person to stand in. (You can also do this inside with masking tape, but check with an adult first to make sure the tape won't harm your flooring!)

3. Hold the clicker and explain to your friends that the goal is to find the correct path through the squares. If they step in a square that is on the path, they will hear a click. If they step in a square that is not on the path, they won't hear anything, and they may then pick another square. Start the timer.

4. Use the grid you drew on the piece of paper to continue playing. If your friend steps in the correct square, click. If he or she steps in the wrong square, don't click.

5. Stop the timer when your friend reaches the end. How long did it take?

6. Repeat steps 1 through 5 to see if your friend can do it faster a second time. Now switch. Take turns by having your friend draw the maze and then you follow the clicks!

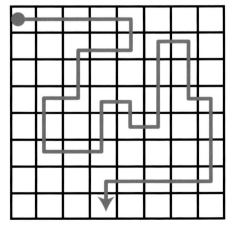

FOR **TEST PREP**, TOO

Another way to practice with the clicker is to use it when you're studying for a spelling or vocabulary test. Give the clicker to the person helping you study. Have him say the word you need to spell or define. If you get it right, he will click. If you get it wrong, he won't click, and you'll need to try again.

The idea is that you will start to associate the sound of the click with something positive. It's a way to reinforce what you've learned as a way to help you succeed. Did you find it helped you study for your test?

DR. GARY'S **VET TIPS**

I recommend always using a clicker with treats, but some cats do not respond to food rewards. If that's the case, you can try rewarding the desired behavior with a favorite toy. Cat grass, a plant that cats find tasty, or catnip, an herb that causes cats to get excited, are fine to use as rewards in limited quantities. Finally, try giving attention as a reward. Some cats will respond to praise, though that's less common with cats than it is with dogs.

BASIC CLICKER
Training

Before you can teach your cat any tricks, she must learn to associate the sound of a clicker with getting a treat. Usually, your cat can learn this in two or three short training sessions.

INSTRUCTIONS

1. Put some treats in a small bowl. Use tiny treats, not large ones, so your cat can eat them quickly without getting full. Bring the bowl of treats to a quiet room and sit on the floor with your cat. You could also sit in a chair with your cat on a table. Hold the clicker in your hand.

2. Let your cat sniff the bowl of treats without letting her eat any. Put the bowl aside. Pick up one treat. Click and at the same time give that one treat to your cat. This is called "charging the clicker." Do not talk while you're doing this.

3. When your cat is done eating the treat, give her another treat while clicking once at the same time. Do it again, but this time, click first and then toss the treat in front of the cat so she has to move to get it. If your cat is agitated or restless, stop and try again during tomorrow's training session. If she's having fun, repeat this five more times, and then end the session.

4. At your next training session, repeat steps 1 through 3. When you click, does your cat look at you expectantly? If she does, that means she has made the connection between the clicker and the treats. If not, try a few more training sessions with her. She should catch on after a few days.

Once you have successfully introduced the clicker, turn the page to learn the next step: teaching your cat how to follow a target. Once your cat responds to the click and can follow a target, you'll be ready to teach her all kinds of tricks!

Follow a
TARGET

Once your cat has learned that when he hears a click he will earn a treat, you can begin adding movement and objects to prepare for further training.

For this trick you will need a target. A target can be anything that you want your cat to focus on. You can purchase a cat training stick called a target stick or a lure stick at a pet shop. Or you can use something in your house, like a tightly capped pen. (Don't use anything with a sharp point that could injure your cat.)

INSTRUCTIONS

❶ Start the session with a click and a treat. Then hold up the target. If your cat moves toward it, click and give him a treat.

❷ Hold up the target again. Click and give him a treat every time he touches it or moves toward it. If he isn't moving, hold the target closer to his face. Click and reward him when he sniffs the target.

❸ Make the activity more challenging for your cat by moving the target away from him and waiting to click and reward him until he goes after it. Repeat this session with your cat until he automatically moves toward the target every time you hold it up.

Your cat will need to know how to follow a target in order to learn most of the tricks in this book.

Removing the Treat

Each trick you'll learn in this book rewards your cat with a click and a treat. But once your cat has mastered the trick, it will be time for you to remove the treat from the process. You will then reward him with a click but no treat. Eventually, you won't even have to click, but you'll still need to use a cue, such as a hand movement or a voice command.

Even though your cat will no longer need a treat for each time he performs, when the entire training session is over, it is always a good idea to offer your feline a treat as a reward for all his hard work.

REMEMBER,
try to do your training
sessions at the same
time every day.

NOT ALL OF THE ACTIVITIES in this chapter require using a clicker. But you want to keep your cat's memory fresh. If you can, try to clicker train your cat every day no matter what, so your cat is always ready for the next click!

CHAPTER 2

BASIC TRAINING

I F YOU'VE reached this chapter, that means you've completed the "Before You Begin" section and introduced clicker training to your cat. If you haven't, stop here and go back to complete chapter 1.

Are you ready to put your best paw forward? While you might be excited to teach your cat some fun things right away, training isn't just about learning tricks. There are some skills your cat needs to know how to do—such as using a litter box—that will help your pet live a healthy life.

Be sure you ask an adult to supervise and then work through this chapter in the order the training is presented, as often one skill helps build toward the next. Of course, if your cat already knows one of the skills, like how to use a litter box, you can skip it and move to the next one. Otherwise, let's take it one skill at a time.

TOOLS
Many activities in this chapter require a few simple items:
▶ A cat training clicker (page 34)
▶ A target stick (page 40)
▶ Cat toys (page 146)
▶ Cat collar (page 48)
▶ Cat carrier (page 52)
▶ Scratching post (page 56)

HANDLING

Cuddle time is learning time. Not all cats enjoy it when you pet them. But it's important to let your cat get used to being touched. This way, he'll be more comfortable when he needs to be groomed or when a vet needs to examine him.

It's always best to get your cat used to being handled when he is just a kitten. But with some patience, you can get an older cat to cooperate, too.

INSTRUCTIONS

1. The best time to try handling your cat is when he is sleepy. Gently pick him up and hold him in your lap.
2. Starting with long, slow strokes pet him starting near his ears and head down his back and sides.

TROUBLESHOOTING: MY CAT WON'T LET ME NEAR HIM!

If you can't even get to step 1 with your cat, don't despair. Try using a clicker and treats. Begin with basic clicker training (page 38) and work with him until he responds to the clicker. Then teach him to come to you on command (page 50).

When he comes to you, reach out and touch him. Click and reward him after you make contact. Take it slowly, and with each session reward him after handling a different part of his body. Eventually, you should be able to handle him.

3. Now check in with your cat. If he is moving around or trying to get away, stop and try again tomorrow. If your cat is calm and purring when you pet him, that's a sign that he's happy being handled. Now you can rub behind his ears and underneath his chin. Do this for about five minutes. Always avoid stroking a cat on his belly! In general only kittens are comfortable with a belly rub, but they grow out of it.
4. If your cat is still calm and happy, touch his legs and pick up each paw one by one. Then move on to his tail. Pet him like this for a few minutes. If it looks like he is uncomfortable, let him go and try again at another time, beginning again with step 1.
5. Once your cat is comfortable being handled, you can practice carrying him. Be sure to use both hands: one under his body and one cradling him. Slowly walk around with him. Hold him firmly but gently so that he cannot jump away. Practice this for at least a few minutes each day.

Once your cat is comfortable being handled by you, you will be ready to move on to some basic training!

A cat's **heart** **beats twice as fast as a human's.**

Using a **LITTER BOX**

It may be a stinky task, but getting your cat to use a litter box is a very important part of training. Because cats have a natural instinct to bury their waste, some will use a litter box right away, without any prompting. Others may need extra help. Either way, once she's mastered this basic skill, your cat will do her business where she should—in the litter box!

INSTRUCTIONS

1 Get a litter box that's about one and a half times as long as your cat. It needs to be roomy enough for her to move around in.

2 Pick one location for the litter box. Do not move it to various places around your house. It should be placed somewhere in your home that gives her some privacy, if possible.

3 Once you've installed the litter box and filled it with litter, bring your cat to it and let her explore it.

4 Put your cat in her litter box five minutes after she eats, or right when she wakes up from a nap. She will get the idea that this is where she's supposed to pee and poo. Repeat this every day until your cat starts to use the litter box on her own.

TROUBLESHOOTING: MY CAT DOESN'T ALWAYS USE THE LITTER BOX!

Do you have more than one cat? If so, you should get more than one litter box. Cats often set up "territories" in a home, and one cat might be keeping another cat out of what it considers to be its litter box territory. If your cat is urinating outside the litter box or spraying urine, check out the training tips on pages 122–125.

WHY DO CATS **BURY THEIR POOP?**

Cat waste has a smell that can attract predators. So cats bury their waste in soft dirt or sand to cover up that scent. Another reason cats cover up their waste is that it might make them sick (through germs and parasites). They make sure to put their droppings in a place far away from their living and sleeping areas, and they bury it for good measure.

Some cats in the wild won't bury their droppings, and scientists think this is because they're marking their territory—or maybe even showing off that they're not afraid of predators.

⚠ SAFETY FIRST

CAT POOP is loaded with germs, so don't ever touch it with your bare hands, and be sure to wash your hands after you clean the litter box.

⚠ SAFETY **FIRST**

ANY COLLAR you put on your cat should be designed specifically for cats. Never tie a ribbon or string around your cat's neck. They are a serious choking hazard for your pet. The best cat collars are "breakaway collars," which have a release on them that will snap open if your cat ever gets her collar caught on something.

When you do fasten the collar, make sure you can fit two fingers between the collar and your cat's neck. If too much of the end of the collar is sticking out after you fasten it, ask an adult to carefully cut it off.

Putting on a **COLLAR**

 Kitty, come home! Even indoor cats can escape outside and get lost, which is why all cats should wear a collar with an ID tag. Even if you have a microchip with your contact information implanted into your cat (which everyone should do!), it's easier for a neighbor to read the tag and call you than it is for them to transport your cat to a vet where the microchip can be read before you are contacted.

We know some cats will sit quietly while you attach a collar around their neck. Others are a bit more reluctant. They might squirm or run away. If that's the case, all you need is some patience, and a few treats, to get that collar clasped.

Make sure you can easily open and close the collar before you try to put it around your kitty's neck.

INSTRUCTIONS

1. Approach your cat in a quiet room with no distractions. Place the collar next to her and let her sniff it for a little bit, so she can see that it's nothing to be afraid of. Give her a treat when she sniffs it.
2. If your cat doesn't run from the collar, try putting it on her. If she lets you do it, congratulations!
3. If you try to put the collar on your cat and she wants no part of it, try it again with a treat in your hand. Let her eat the treat while you fasten the collar. Repeat this five times and then try it without the treat.

DR. GARY'S **VET TIPS**

Give it time. If your cat still doesn't let you put the collar on, give her a treat while holding the collar open around her neck without fastening it. Then take the collar away. Do this about a dozen times over two days, and it should work!

COME

Here, kitty, kitty! In the basic clicker training activity (page 38), your cat learned that if she made contact with a target, she would be rewarded with a click and a treat.

Now it's time to add a verbal, or spoken, command. According to some experts, "Come" is the most basic command every cat needs to know. Once you and your cat master this, you should be able to tackle other tricks more easily.

INSTRUCTIONS

1. Hold up a target (page 40) and say "Come." Your cat should start to walk to the target. If she does, click and give her a treat. Repeat this three to five times.
2. Now move to a different spot, or take a few steps back. Hold up the target and say "Come." If she does, click and reward her. Do this at least five times. If she doesn't, try again at your next session.

Advanced

Once your cat will come when she sees the target, try it without a target. You may need to practice for a full week or longer before you can attempt this. Hold up your hand and say "Come." Click and reward her each time she comes to you on command. Repeat this at least five times.

IF YOUR CAT STARTS TO WALK to the target and you haven't said "Come," ignore her. Don't click or give her a treat. Turn your head. Then try the trick again starting at step 2.

Getting Into a
CAT CARRIER

Cats love to climb in boxes, so why are they so afraid of cat carriers? It's because your cat knows that this box is used only when he's going to the vet, and he probably hates that. So when he sees the carrier, he runs.

The best thing you can do is to make the carrier a safe place for your cat to hang out anytime. Leave the carrier open in the room your cat plays in the most. Then, when it's time to go to the vet, he will hop in as he always does.

INSTRUCTIONS

1. If you have a hard-plastic carrier, remove the top and the front door. To make it cozy, put a small cat bed, soft blanket, or towel in the carrier. Add a favorite toy. Leave the carrier in your cat's favorite room.

2. Put some treats inside the carrier. Most cats will venture in to get the treats. Repeat this for a few days so that your cat gets used to going into the carrier on his own.

3. Next, try picking him up and placing him in the carrier. If you succeed, give him a treat and pet him. If he struggles, don't force him. Try again the next day.

4. Repeat step 3 every day until your cat goes in easily without a struggle. Now, put the top and door back onto your hard carrier. The door might swing back and forth and scare your cat, so tape the door all the way open with strong tape—so it can't swing and the door is flush against the side of the carrier. Once your cat is inside, shut the door (or zip it closed if you are using a soft carrier). If your cat starts to panic, let him out. If he stays calm, keep him inside for five minutes before letting him out. Repeat this for a week.

5. Put him back in the carrier from time to time to make sure your cat stays used to it. Leave the carrier out all the time so your cat can explore it whenever he wants to.

The next time you need to take your cat to the vet—or anywhere else outside your home—guide him into the crate.

DR. GARY'S **VET TIPS**

It's an emergency, and you haven't had time yet to train your cat to get in his carrier. What can you do? The important thing to remember is to never fight your cat to get her into a carrier.

First, quietly and carefully set up the carrier on a tabletop. If your cat hears the carrier door bang open, she may bolt and hide.

If you have a hard-sided carrier, you can try to take off its top, place the cat on the bottom, and close the top over her when she settles down. Even better, use a soft-sided carrier, which is much less threatening than a box with bars. Throw in treats and a toy and a thick towel to hide under. When picking up the carrier, always hold it from the bottom, and never by the top handle. That would create a swinging ride your cat wouldn't appreciate!

You may also want to purchase in advance one of the natural pheromone-based sprays available that help calm down cats. Use the spray directly on the carrier, and it may help your cat feel less afraid.

Using a **CAT DOOR**

A cat door is an opening small enough to let your cat go in and out of rooms, but not big enough for a dog or a person to fit through. You might use a cat door to let your cat access a room where she can go to feel safe when things get hectic in your home. Or the cat door might lead to the room where her litter box is kept.

If you would like your cat to use a cat door, she might figure it out on her own if she's really interested in finding out what's on the other side. If not, it shouldn't take long before she gets the hang of it.

INSTRUCTIONS

1. Cat doors have a flap over the opening that must be pushed to get through. To make your cat comfortable with going through the flap, hold it open with your hands when you introduce your kitty to the door.

2. While your cat watches, put your hand through the door and hold treats on the other side.

3. Let her poke just her head through to get to the treats. She doesn't need to climb all the way through the door. Repeat this three times.

4. Now, toss the treats through the door. Your cat should have to pass through the opening to retrieve them. Repeat this three times.

5. The next time you toss the treats through the door, hold the flap so that it is only partly covering the door. Make sure the flap doesn't accidentally hit your cat, or she may get frightened. Repeat tossing the treats, holding the flap a little more closed each time. After a few tries, she'll get used to pushing the flap and will do it on her own.

SHOULD YOU LET YOUR CAT **OUTSIDE?**

Most vets say "No way!" Between cars and dogs and other threats, the outdoors can be dangerous for your cat. There is also the risk that she could get sick or injured or be unable to find her way home. If your kitty really wants to go outside, ask an adult for permission to take her on a walk (see page 80). That will be good exercise for both of you!

Using a
SCRATCHING POST

Claws of destruction! Plenty of cat owners have come home to find the family couch or curtains ripped to shreds by their cat. Your cat isn't doing this because she's bad. She's simply displaying a natural behavior and using what's available to her.

In the wild, your cat would scratch her claws on a tree. In your home, she'll find the next best thing. Instead of letting her claw your house apart, get her to use a scratching post!

INSTRUCTIONS

1. Choose a scratching post. Many types are available in pet stores or online. Some are made of corrugated cardboard and can be replaced when they wear out. Some are logs or pieces of wood. Other cat posts are covered in household carpeting or a roughly textured rope called sisal.

2. Set up your scratching post. Many cats like to scratch and stretch when they wake up, so set it up next to your cat's sleeping area if possible.

3. Carry your cat to the post. If she scratches the post, reward her with a treat. Repeat this at least five times and continue until she starts to use it on her own, without your prompting her.

4. If your cat doesn't scratch the post, try putting some toys or favorite treats near the base to entice her. You can even try putting some catnip on or around the post. Repeat this each day until she uses it on her own.

YOU MAY HAVE TO TRY A FEW different types of scratching posts before you find the kind your cat likes best. Fortunately, scratching posts come in all shapes and sizes!

TROUBLESHOOTING:
MY CAT IS STILL SCRATCHING THE FURNITURE

Your cat might still scratch something off-limits, even after you've introduced the scratching post. If you catch her doing this, interrupt her by firmly saying "No." Then pick her up and move her to the scratching post. Do this every time you catch her in the act. Do not yell at her, and never hit her.

WHY DO CATS **SCRATCH?**

Out in the wild, cats like to mark their territory so that other cats know to stay away. When they scratch, glands in their paws release a scent, which acts as an invisible sign saying, "There is a cat who lives around here!"

But that's not the only reason why cats need to scratch. Scratching is good exercise that allows them to stretch their bodies and claws. Also, those claws are covered by a protective outer layer as they grow. Scratching helps the cat remove that old layer so the new one can replace it.

57

TOUCH and PLAY Ball

Break time! Your cat has been working hard with you on all kinds of basic training. Take some time to teach him a playful trick. Train your cat to pick up a ball in his mouth and he'll be ready for some of the more difficult moves later in this book.

INSTRUCTIONS

1. Grab a ball or another toy that your cat can easily fit in his mouth and that he already likes to play with. Don't use anything that he can accidentally swallow.
2. Move close to your cat. Hold the ball a few inches in front of his nose.
3. When he makes contact with the ball, click and reward him with a treat.
4. Next, pull the ball away. Repeat steps 1 through 4 at least five times.
5. The next time your cat touches the ball, don't click and reward him unless he puts his mouth on it. It may take him a few tries and different ways of touching the ball before he figures this out. Repeat this at least five more times or until your cat grabs the ball with his mouth every time. If this doesn't happen on the first day of practice, don't give up! Repeat the steps for a couple of days until he gets the hang of it.

Bezoar is the scientific name for a hair ball.

Keep Your Cat
CALM AT THE VET

Training your cat to keep calm at the vet is very important. It's natural for your cat to be frightened of a place with new people and strange smells. But as his owner, you can do a few things to keep his vet visit as stress free as possible.

- If there is a choice of vets in your area, work with the adults in your family to try to find one with a good cat-side manner! Ask other cat owners for recommendations.

- Introduce your cat to a cat carrier before he needs to go to a vet (page 52). That way, when it's time to go, he'll be ready. This would also be a good time to try using that calming spray on the carrier.

- When you walk with the carrier, be sure to keep it steady. Do not hold the carrier by its handle! Carry it with both arms to keep it balanced and the ride smooth as you transport your pet.

- If you're using a car to get to the vet, play soothing music during the ride. The key is to give your cat a calm environment for the whole journey. Also, you might want to take him on short car rides before he needs to go to the vet to get him familiar with it—the same way you got him used to going into the carrier. This will help make him more comfortable in the car when he really needs to go somewhere.

- If your vet's office has a "No Dogs" area, sit there while you wait. If the office is filled with dogs and other noisy animals, wait outside with your cat until it's time for his appointment. In any case, don't take your cat out of the carrier until you are in the room with the doctor.

Cats on CAMERA

Anyone who thinks it's impossible to train cats simply needs to turn on the TV or watch a movie. In a television commercial when a cat runs to a bowl and begins to eat—that's a trained cat. A movie cat chasing a bad guy across the screen—that's a trained cat.

Most professional cat trainers use clicker training, just like you are learning to do in this book. They teach cats basic commands like "Stay" and "Come," as well as specific commands they need for their acting role.

Sometimes, multiple cats that look alike play the same role in a film. That's because one cat might be better at jumping, while another might be better at keeping still while being held. Also, if one cat gets tired and needs a rest, her co-star can take over. Different cats may be used for each scene, depending on her strengths. Because they look so similar, the audience thinks it's always the same cat.

Here's how these famous cats got into the act:

Pepper

This feline is considered the first cat actor. She was born under the floor of a movie studio in 1912 and crawled up through the floorboards while a movie scene was being filmed. She went on to appear in 17 films and even worked with the legendary actor Charlie Chaplin.

Morris

Many orange tabbies have played Morris, the star of commercials for 9Lives cat food, since his debut on-screen in 1969. The first cat to play the role was rescued from a humane society in Illinois, U.S.A., by an animal trainer. The cat's name? Lucky!

Crookshanks

If you've seen the Harry Potter movies, then you know that Hermione Granger's pet is a cat named Crookshanks. Several Persian cats played the role, but one named Crackerjack was the best at performing on command. No matter what his trainer needed him to do, Crackerjack did it well.

CROOKSHANKS

PEPPER

MORRIS

(A+) Time for a **CHECK-IN!**

Great job so far! If you've gotten to this point in the book, that means you have put in some serious time with your cat. Congratulate yourself for being a thoughtful and caring pet owner.

Moving forward, you'll be learning how to teach your cat some cool tricks, as well as to correct your kitty's unwanted behaviors. To make sure you're ready to move on, ask yourself these questions:

- Do you practice with your cat almost every day? If not, try to train more frequently.
- Does your cat respond to the clicker when you use it? If not, go back to practice clicker training (page 38) before you move on.

- Is your cat calm and happy during training sessions or stressed out? If your cat is stressed out, make sure that you are training in a quiet place with no distractions or other animals present.

Now that you've checked in, it's time to pounce into the "Intermediate Tricks and Training" section!

At one formal White House dinner, President **Abraham Lincoln fed his cat** Tabby from the table.

DR. GARY'S **TRAINING TIPS**

Some cats will learn only a few basic commands—and that's OK! It's a huge accomplishment to teach your cat even these basic skills, and he'll be much better behaved because of it. Well done!

CHAPTER 3

INTERMEDIATE
TRICKS AND
TRAINING

YOU'VE SEEN DOGS "Sit" and "Shake," but what about our feline friends? Can they be copycats? You bet! To perform these tricks, your cat needs to know clicker training (page 38). Try one trick before moving on to the next. If your cat just can't master a trick, skip it!

TOOLS
You'll need a few simple items to complete some of the activities in this chapter:

▶ A cat training clicker (page 34)

▶ A target stick (page 40)

▶ Cat treats (page 35)

▶ Cat toys (page 146)

▶ A harness and leash (page 80)

DON'T FORGET!

▶ Work with your cat in a quiet room free from distractions.

▶ Ask an adult to supervise.

▶ Start each session with a refresher: click and a treat.

▶ Stop the training if your cat gets agitated.

▶ Never yell at or harm your cat.

▶ End each training session with a treat.

SHAKE

Pleased to meet you, kitty! Once your cat is comfortable with her paws being touched, you can teach her to shake hands on command. Or, OK, shake paws!

INSTRUCTIONS

1. Gently pick up one of your cat's paws with your hand.
2. With your other hand, click and at the very same time say "Shake."
3. Reward your cat with a treat while still holding her paw.
4. Let go of her paw. Pet and praise her.
5. Repeat steps 1 through 4 at least five times. Be sure to use the same paw and hand each time.
6. When your cat begins to master this skill, give the command, offer your hand, and wait for her to lift up her paw on her own. When she does, touch her paw with your hand, and then click and reward her. Repeat this five times.
7. If she doesn't lift her paw on her own after you say "Shake," do it for her. Then click and give her a treat. Repeat this until she lifts her paw on her own every time you offer your hand.

CAT TALES

A Russian white kitten named Jasmine has perfect manners. As soon as her owner reaches for her paw, she stands up on two legs and shakes his hand every time.

Q: Not *feline* well?
A: Maybe you need to call a *purr*-amedic.

BEG

OK, so teaching a cat to beg is not super useful. But it's a great party trick that's sure to make your friends smile. Plus, it will help you prove that cats can do anything dogs can do!

INSTRUCTIONS

1. Hold a treat under your kitty's nose, but don't give it to him.
2. Move the treat up so it is raised a few inches over his head and away from his body.
3. As your kitty stands on his hind legs and reaches for the reward, click and offer the treat. Repeat this at least five times.
4. Once your cat can do this trick with the click and the treat, try to train him using the voice command. Hold up the treat, and say "Beg." Click and give him the treat as he stands. Repeat this at least five times. Eventually, he should respond to the command when you raise your hand and say "Beg" even if you don't have a treat in your hand.

This command can also be taught using the word "Up" for when you want your cat to stand on his hind legs for you.

CAT TALES

Nicole the cat loves berries! She comes running when she hears the crinkly sound of a plastic clamshell berry box. Then she stands up and meows loudly until she's offered some berries.

A group of
CATS
is called a
CLOWDER.

SIT

"Sit" is another classic command that is associated with dogs, but it can be a useful thing to teach a cat. Some cats have a knack of being in the way when a room becomes chaotic, and a "Sit" command can help calm things down.

INSTRUCTIONS

1. Bring a treat up to your cat's nose, but don't give it to her.
2. Slowly move up your hand behind your cat's head a bit so that your cat lowers her body into a sitting position. This can be tricky, so experiment with the position of the treat until your cat sits. Whatever you do, don't push her into place. Also, do not hold the treat too high; you don't want your cat to jump for it.
3. When she sits, click and give her the treat.
4. Repeat steps 1 through 3 at least five times.
5. After your cat can successfully sit, add the verbal command. Say "Sit" whenever you hold the treat above her head. When she sits, click and give her the treat. Repeat this at least five times.

Advanced

After your cat has responded to the command "Sit" for at least a week, try adding a hand signal. The next time you give the command "Sit," do not use treats or the clicker. Instead, use the hand that would have held the treats and open your palm so it is flat and facing the floor. Repeat this at least five times. With practice, she should respond to the command with the hand signal and won't need the click or the treat. But you should still reinforce this trick with a treat from time to time.

DR. GARY'S **TRAINING TIPS**

Teaching a cat to sit is relatively easy and can be very useful for when you need to give her medicine, brush her teeth, or keep her away from something threatening or dangerous.

STAY

Once your cat learns to sit on command, you can try to teach him to remain in one place for a short period of time until you release him.

INSTRUCTIONS

1. Start by giving your cat the "Sit" command (page 72).
2. Once he's sitting, wave at your cat with one hand—this is just a test to see whether he'll be distracted by the movement. If he still sits, click and offer a treat. Repeat this at least five times. If he moves, then ask him to sit again and keep trying until he figures out that he won't get the treat unless he sits still. If he's still moving after five tries, stop and work on this again tomorrow. If your cat is able to sit still when you wave your hand, move on to the next step.
3. Take three small steps back. Does he move? If not, click and give him a treat. Repeat this five times.
4. As you continue, gradually move farther and farther away. Repeat steps 1 through 3, but then take a few more steps each time. If your cat moves, don't scold him. Just put him back in place and start again. Repeat this at least five times.
5. Now add the verbal command. Tell him "Stay" and then move away. If he stays, click and offer a treat. Repeat this at least five times.

Advanced

Once your cat masters "Stay," add a release command such as "OK" so that he knows that he can start moving again. You can teach this command with your clicker. Say "OK" and then click and give him a treat when he moves. Repeat this every time you say "Stay."

DR. GARY'S **VET TIPS**

Teaching a cat to stay is much more difficult than teaching him to sit—and some cats will never do it. If your cat won't stay after a week of training, don't get frustrated with him or force him to stay. Just move on to the next trick!

THINK ABOUT
applying the command "Stay" to
useful situations. For example, if your
cat weaves around your feet while
you are making lunch, you can tell
him to stay until you are finished.

SPEAK

When you train your cat to speak, it means training her to meow on cue. Soon you'll be making beautiful *meow*-sic with your cat!

INSTRUCTIONS

1. You'll want to start talking to your cat. Begin by saying the word "meow."

2. Repeat the word "meow" until your cat meows back. As soon as she does, click and give her a treat. Repeat this at least five times.

3. If your cat doesn't meow back at all, don't give up. Try again in your next training session and keep at it for at least a week and see what happens. If she's just not interested, move on to the next trick.

4. If your cat does meow back, add a command. Say "Speak," and then say "Meow." Click and reward her when she responds. Repeat this five times.

Advanced

Now drop the word "meow" and say only "Speak." Click and reward her when she responds. If she doesn't respond, repeat "Speak" a few times to see if she will do it.

WHY DO CATS **MEOW?**

Kittens will meow to get the attention of their mothers, but adult cats do not meow to each other at all. To communicate, they use body language, facial expressions, scent, and touch. Scientists believe that cats started meowing at humans because we didn't understand their "language." So they meow to tell us what they want and need.

Your cat will usually meow to tell you she is hungry or wants something from you, such as a toy or a scratch. Sometimes a meow just means hello. And sometimes, it's a cry of pain or distress.

The important thing to remember is that if your cat is making noise, pay attention. If you're not sure what she wants, try to read what her body language is telling you (page 24).

One reason **cats lick** their fur is to **cool down** in hot weather. The saliva evaporates and **lowers** their body temperature.

🐾 CAT TALES

Mari had been living with a foster family that had dogs. When Mari arrived in her forever home, her owners noticed their new pet acted more like a dog than a cat. She'd wait at the window for her owner to get home from work, greet her at the door, then roll on her back for a belly rub!

Roll OVER

With this trick, you will let the good times roll! It will take some patience and repetition to master, but it's impressive once you've got it down. Before attempting this trick, your cat must be able to respond to the "Sit" command (page 72).

INSTRUCTIONS

1. You'll want to practice this trick on the floor. Set your cat down and kneel or sit comfortably in front of him. Tell your cat "Sit."

2. Put a treat in front of his nose, but don't let him eat it.

3. Slowly move the treat to the left side of his body. The idea is to get him to turn his head so that he can reach the treat. But don't let him get it!

4. Then slowly move the treat down to the floor. You want your cat to lie on his side, with his eyes facing the treat. When you do this, say "Roll over." He should try to roll his body so that he can reach the treat. Do not click and give him the treat until he rolls over. This might happen quickly, so be ready with your treat. Repeat this at least five times.

5. To finish the trick, hold a treat in front of your cat's nose while he is lying on the floor. Say "OK" to release him and slowly move the treat up and to the right so that he follows it back into a sitting or standing position. Make sure to click and reward him when he's back up. Repeat this at this least five times.

6. Now combine all the steps so that your cat completes the roll.

DR. GARY'S VET TIPS

This trick might take several days or even a few weeks to perfect, so don't get discouraged if it doesn't happen right away. If he won't roll over on day one, start the steps all over again during your next training session.

Wear a
HARNESS

Ready to take your cat for a walk? Before you can both go outside, you need to start training inside. And that means getting your cat used to wearing a harness.

Every cat should wear a collar with an ID tag in case she goes missing. But if you want to walk your cat on a leash, you'll need a harness. The harness must attach to her back, and not around her neck, as this could cause injury. The key to getting your cat comfortable with the harness—and eventually the leash—it to take away her fear of it. That may require several days, but it's worth the time.

INSTRUCTIONS

1. Before you attempt to put the harness on your cat, you'll want to introduce her to it. Leave the harness out for her to discover it. Put it near her bed or in an area where she likes to play. Leave it out for a few days.
2. Drape the harness over your cat without securing any of the clasps. Let her feel it. Take it off and put it on her at least five times.
3. You will know that your cat is comfortable having the harness touch her fur when she no longer runs away from it or flinches to move it off immediately. Once your kitty reaches this step, try to secure the harness.
4. Offer your kitty a treat while you're attaching the harness securely. Leave it on her for a short time—about five minutes—at first. When you remove it, give

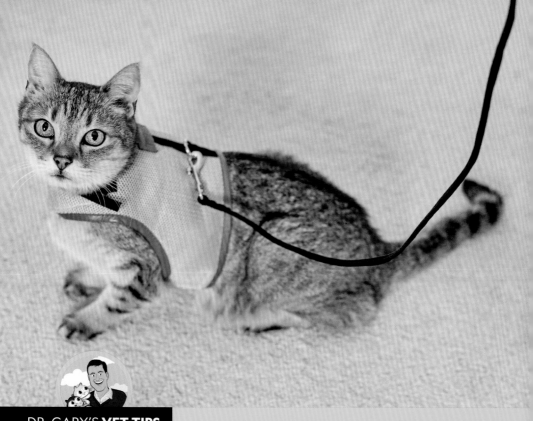

Before you go outside, ask yourself these questions: Does my cat have all her shots? Does my cat have protection from fleas and ticks?

If the answer is no to either of these questions, talk to your vet before you head outdoors. Even though you'll be walking her on a leash, she won't be protected from diseases, insects, or other cats.

her another treat. Great job! Your cat can wear a harness.

5 Repeat step 4 once a day for three days. Each day, see if you can leave the harness on a little longer. Once you can leave it on for 30 minutes without your cat becoming agitated, move to the next step.

6 Attach a six-foot (1.8-m) leash to the harness. Let your cat move around inside the house only, with the harness and leash attached.

Supervise her at all times to make sure that the leash does not get tangled on something. Spend five minutes walking her inside the house for at least three days, or until she seems really comfortable on the leash.

7 Once your cat has mastered step 6, you're almost ready to start walking her outside. Turn to the next page to find out how.

Walk on a LEASH

Let's safely explore the great outdoors! Most cats love being outside, but the danger of their being harmed by disease, predators, or even other cats is too great to let them roam free. The safest way to let your cat experience nature is to teach her how to walk on a leash. Always be sure your cat is wearing a collar with an ID and has a microchip implanted by your vet before you take her outside—even on a leash! Ask an adult for permission before you head outside.

Your cat must have completed the harness training (page 80) before you attempt this activity. Remember that your leash should be no longer than six feet (1.8 m), so your cat won't get too far ahead of you.

Wear long sleeves and pants in case your cat gets frightened outside and jumps up on you. Then follow these steps to take a stroll with your kitty.

INSTRUCTIONS

1 Before you take your cat outside, stay inside and teach her how to stop. If she tries to run or pull on the leash, stop walking. Don't move again until she also stops. (You can also give her the "Sit" command on page 72.) When you're ready to move again, tell her "Let's go," and start to walk. Click and give her a treat as well as lots of praise when she succeeds. Repeat this anytime she tries to run or pull away.

2 Try to choose a quiet location for your first walk outside. It's natural for your cat to act fearful. Your cat might try to go back inside or climb up into your arms. Or she might hunker down and refuse to move. That's fine! Don't force her to walk. Try again another time.

3 When you are walking your cat outside, keeping her safe is your number one priority. Stay beside her and keep your eyes on her at all times. Do not let her pick up anything and put it in her mouth. Don't let her climb up trees or other objects. Do not tie her leash to something and walk away.

4 Keep your first few walks very short—stay out for no more than 10 minutes. After five short walks on different days, you may want to extend your walks, making them longer each time.

DR. GARY'S **VET TIPS**

Training your cat to walk on a leash is a wonderful alternative to letting your cat go outside on her own. Cats really want to go outside. It's unnatural for them to stay indoors all their lives. They want to explore and see the world, and a harness is a safe way to allow them to do this. Watch out, though: Once your cat gets a taste of the outdoors, she may beg you to take her out multiple times a day!

SOCIAL MEDIA Sensations

Cute kitty videos! Everybody loves them and shares them. Here are a few of the most famous felines on the internet:

Maru

Maru is a chubby, fluffy, gray-and-white Scottish fold who lives in Japan. When Maru was a kitten, his owner decided to start taking photos and videos of him. In 2008, the owner posted a video of Maru sliding across the floor and jumping into an impossibly tiny box. The video went viral, and a star was born. Today, Maru's videos have more than 325 million views.

Honey Bee

Sometimes cats become famous because their stories are inspiring. That's what happened to Honey Bee, a blind cat from the island of Fiji, in the South Pacific.

Honey Bee was living in an animal shelter when she was adopted and brought back to Washington State, U.S.A. Her new owners began taking Honey Bee on hikes with them, walking her on a leash. Honey Bee would jump up on their shoulders to be carried when she got tired and then squirm when she wanted to walk again. She would sniff the air and stop to listen to the sounds of nature. She would take water and food breaks, and when it was time to go back home, she would curl up in a pet sling and sleep.

In 2014, Honey Bee's owners posted a video of her hiking, and soon everybody was talking about the blind cat who found a new life climbing mountains.

Grumpy Cat

Her owners knew her as Tardar Sauce, but you may have known her as Grumpy Cat. Before she passed away in 2019, she had more than 8.3 million followers on one social media site.

Grumpy Cat was a mixed-breed cat with a condition called feline dwarfism, which means she was smaller than most adult cats. And her face always looked like it was frowning. Her unique looks made her a sensation after her photo and videos were posted on social media.

Not every cat can make it as a social media celebrity. But the lesson of Grumpy Cat is this: Your cat doesn't have to be a master of tricks to be special. Every cat is lovable in her own way. Spend time with your pet to find out what makes her your superstar.

ADVANCED
TRICKS AND
TRAINING

C AN YOUR CAT perform complicated tricks? Some cats are easier to train than others, and it's possible your cat might be a master! Or perhaps he is not cut out to perform these challenging moves. Before you give up on him make sure you complete chapters 2 and 3. Give your cat regular training sessions. Then give these tricks a try.

Grab an adult and do the activities in order, because they build on one another. If your cat can't do a trick, skip it and try a different one. He may surprise you!

DON'T FORGET!

▶ Work with your cat in a quiet room free from distractions.

▶ Start each session with a click and a treat so that he remembers to associate the click with the treat.

▶ Stop the training if your cat gets agitated.

▶ Never yell at or harm your cat.

TOOLS

▶ A cat training clicker (page 34)

▶ A target stick (page 40)

▶ Cat treats (page 35)

▶ Cat toys (page 146)

▶ Two chairs

▶ A service bell

▶ A tissue box

▶ A dangling cat toy or cat agility bar

▶ A Hula-Hoop or cat training hoop

▶ A paper bag or cat agility tunnel

FETCH

Go get it, kitty! Let's face it—toss a ball and most dogs will happily bound after it and bring it back to you. Most cats—well, they don't care about chasing after a ball. But there is a kind of cat that excels at fetch: an active cat that loves toys. If that sounds like your cat, then go ahead and give this trick a try!

Before you teach this command, your cat must be able to do the Touch and Play Ball trick (page 58) and respond to the "Come" command (page 50).

INSTRUCTIONS

❶ Start with the Touch and Play Ball trick. Repeat it three times.

❷ Now, show your cat the ball. Place the ball on the floor instead of holding it in your hand. Click and reward him when he grabs the ball in his mouth. Repeat this at least five times.

❸ Encourage your cat to move around with the ball in his mouth. Tap on the floor with your hand, or verbally talk to him to get him moving. Click and reward him when he picks it up and moves with it. Do not click and reward him unless he does this. Repeat this at least five times.

❹ Move the ball a short distance away. When your cat picks it up, say "Come." Click and reward him when he comes to you. Repeat this five times.

Expert

After your cat consistently brings the ball to you, add a command. We recommend not adding the command until the second week of daily practice, since fetch is a complicated trick. Begin tossing the ball instead of simply placing it away from you. When he reaches the ball, say "Fetch."

A cat's
brain weighs
as much as
five quarters.

There are programs **teaching shelter cats** how to **high-five.** This simple trick helps **increase** their chance of **being adopted.**

NO LUCK?
If you get to step 6 and your cat doesn't confidently hive-five the container, stop and work on steps 1 through 5 for a week before moving on.

High-**FIVE**

 All the coolest cats know this trick. Teaching your cat to high-five on cue is a surefire way to impress your friends and family. This trick also comes in handy when you or a vet need to handle your cat's paws. Before attempting this activity, your cat must be able to respond to the "Sit" command (page 72).

INSTRUCTIONS

1. Command your cat to sit. Click and reward him with a treat.
2. Hold a small container of treats in one hand and the clicker in the other. The container will be used as the target for this training.
3. Let your cat sniff the container, and then raise it above his head.
4. Your curious cat should raise his paw to investigate what's in your hand. Click as soon as he does that. Then give him the treat.
5. Repeat steps 1 through 4 at least 10 times. At first, your cat might raise his paw without touching the target. That's OK; you can click and reward him when he does that. But as you repeat, withhold the treat until he raises his paw a little higher each time. Continue until his paw touches the container, and then click and give him

a treat. Congratulations! Your cat has figured out a basic high five.

6. If your pet has mastered the above steps, continue by removing the target (the treat container) from your hand right before the cat's paw touches it. Repeat this 10 times, and then gradually phase out the container. Open your palm, high-five style, when he reaches for it. As soon as your cat begins to reach for your hand, say "High-five."

7. Click and give him a treat when his paw touches your hand. Keep practicing until he recognizes the command—and don't reward him if he tries to high-five you without the command. Once he's mastered the skill, he should be able to perform it with the verbal cue only.

TROUBLESHOOTING: MY CAT WON'T TOUCH MY HAND!

If treats won't entice your cat to raise his paw, swap out the container for his favorite toy. Hold the toy in your hand so that he can see it. Click and reward him if he reaches for it. As you repeat the training, gradually pull the toy into your hand so that he will reach for your hand even when nothing is in it.

WAVE

Imagine this: As you're leaving for school, you turn and wave to your cat.

"Goodbye, Bella!" you call out, and your cat waves back.

That's a great way to start your day, and a social media moment for sure. But this is a difficult trick to teach. So take a deep breath before starting. It will likely take a lot of practice to teach your cat this very advanced trick.

Before you begin, your cat must be able to respond to the "High-five" command (page 90).

INSTRUCTIONS

1. Place your cat someplace where she can see your hand when you wave to her, such as on a sofa or chair.
2. Cue your cat to high-five. Click and reward her.
3. Now slowly take two baby steps away from her and cue her to high-five again. Don't move too fast, or she might jump off the chair. You should be close, but too far away for her to touch your hand. If she raises her paw, click and reward her. Repeat five times, moving two steps each time.

4. Now it's time to replace the "High-five" cue with a hand signal. Wiggle your fingers or wave. Click and reward your cat if she raises her paw when you do this.
5. Keep practicing this trick, moving farther away each time, until she responds to your signal to wave from across the room.

The statue of a waving cat is a Japanese lucky charm. Tradition says that if its right paw is raised, the cat will protect your home.

If the left paw is raised, the cat will bring you good business.

92

Ring a BELL

Ding! Oh, that's my cat, who rings a bell when he wants a treat. So cool, right? But be warned: This cute trick can become annoying really quickly if your cat rings the bell over ... and over ... and over again. You may have to hide the bell to find some peace and quiet.

If you don't mind a little noise and want to try this trick, you'll need what's known as a service bell: a round metal bell with a push button on the top. When you push the button, the bell dings.

INSTRUCTIONS

1. Place your cat on a chair and kneel or sit so that you are level with him.
2. Put the bell on top of a small box, such as a tissue box, so that your cat has to reach for it.
3. Place your cat in front of the box.
4. Put a treat in your hand and place your hand on the side of the bell that is farthest away from your cat.
5. Click and reward your cat if he reaches for your hand. At this point, he'll be putting his paw over the bell but not neces-sarily on it. Repeat this five times.

6. Remove the box and click and reward him only when his paw touches the top of the bell instead of your hand.
7. After he's figured out how to place his paw on the bell, continue to click and reward him only when he touches the button. Repeat this at least five times.
8. After he's mastered touching the button, reward him only when he puts enough pressure on the button so that it makes a sound. Ding! By now your cat should be ringing the bell. Only click and reward him when the bell rings. At this point, he should ring the bell on his own every time you put it in front of him.

You may have heard the term **"tomcat"** used for a male cat. But what is a female cat called? **A queen!**

95

CRAWL
Through a Tunnel

Ladies and gentlemen, boys and girls, behold the amazing tunneling cat! While this trick may look like something you'd see in a circus act, the truth is that most cats are willing to do it without too much coaxing. You can find a cat agility tunnel in a pet shop, or make one yourself. Simply grab an adult and have them help you cut the bottoms off two or three paper bags and tape them together, end to end. Make sure the bags are wide enough for your cat to fit through comfortably. Voilà— a tunnel!

INSTRUCTIONS

1. Set up the tunnel on the floor. To begin, you want a tunnel that's no longer than three feet (1 m), so that your cat can clearly see you when you are on one side and she's on the other.

2. Place your cat next to the tunnel. If she seems afraid of it, then leave it out for a few days until she gets used to it. If she seems curious, place a few treats inside the tunnel. She will likely go inside it to get them.

3. Next, put your cat at one end of the tunnel. Position yourself at the other end. Wave or wiggle a target. She will run through the tunnel to get to the target. Click and reward her.

4. Repeat steps 2 and 3 at least five times, switching your position so that your cat goes through the tunnel from both ends.

Expert

You can create a longer tunnel for your cat by putting two or more tunnels together. She may be confident enough to enter a longer tunnel because she knows she will be rewarded at the other end!

Feline fans celebrate **National Cat Day** every year on **October 29.**

CAT TALES

Some cats are natural jumpers. Luna jumps all over the furniture in her home like a kitty parkour artist. She even gets her claws into the couch and hangs upside down with her head tilted to the side, like Spider-Man!

JUMP

In the wild, cats climb up trees and over walls as they explore the world around them to search for prey or to escape predators. That makes them naturally good jumpers. So you don't need to teach them to jump, but what you can do is teach them to jump on or over things on command.

INSTRUCTIONS

1. Grab your target (page 40). Also find a stick that is long enough for your cat to jump over when you hold it horizontally—the kind of stick attached to a dangling cat toy works great. You can also purchase an agility bar made especially for cats.

2. Place the long stick on the ground for him to step over. Move the target over the stick to see if your cat will follow it. The idea here is to get him to go over the stick. Place a treat on the other side of the stick if he doesn't step over it on his own. You can also replace the target you're using with a toy or a treat. Once he does step over the stick, click and reward him. Repeat this five times.

3. Now grab an adult and have them help you hold the long stick with one hand so that it is horizontal to the floor. Raise it so the stick it is suspended off the floor by a few inches, and hold the stick steady. Move the target over the stick and see if your cat will follow. Click and reward him every time he steps over the stick. Repeat this five times.

4. Experiment by raising the target a little bit higher each time. Your cat should jump over the stick to reach the target.

5. Add a command to this trick. Say "Jump" when you hold up the target as you're luring him over the stick. Repeat this at least five times. Once he's mastered the skill, he should be able to perform it with the verbal cue only.

DR. GARY'S **VET TIPS**

Most cats are pretty agile, even when they get older, but that doesn't mean they can do any trick. Most cats get arthritis as they age, just as humans do, so it's important to know your cat and know what he's capable of doing. If you have a senior cat, you might want to let him step over the stick instead of jump over it.

JUMP
Through a Hoop

It will take repetition and patience to pull off this trick, but the results are impressive!

Make sure there are no fragile or dangerous items nearby that your cat could knock over. Your cat will need to have mastered the "Jump" command (page 98) before doing this trick.

INSTRUCTIONS

1. Find a small, simple hoop for this trick. A child-size Hula-Hoop can work, as long as it doesn't light up or make a noise that could startle your cat. You can also purchase an animal training hoop at a pet store. Make sure the hoop is large enough for your cat to fit through it comfortably. We don't want him getting stuck!

2. Place the hoop on the floor and let your cat sniff and explore it. If you need to, leave it around for a few days so your cat can get comfortable with it before continuing.

3. Stand up the hoop with the bottom touching the floor. Use your cat's favorite target to lure him through the hoop. Click and reward him when he steps through it. Repeat this at least five times.

4. Raise the hoop one inch (2.5 cm) above the floor. Hold the target on the other side of the hoop.

5. Click and reward your cat when he walks through the hoop—but not if he goes around the hoop or tries to go under it. Repeat this at least five times.

6. Raise the hoop another inch. Click and reward your cat when he walks through the hoop. Repeat this at least five times.

7. Add a command. Say "Jump" when you hold up the target. With practice, your cat will jump through the hoop when you say the command and you won't need the target anymore.

Expert

If your kitty loves to jump, you can add an extra element to this trick by having your cat jump from one surface or another with a hoop in the middle. To teach your cat this, first he'll need to learn the Jump From Chair to Chair trick (page 102), to which you'll add the hoop.

DR. GARY'S **VET TIPS**

How high should you go? You always want your cat to be safe when doing acrobatic tricks like this one or jump on page 98. You can raise the hoop or stick a few inches, but don't go too high. Take the cue from your cat and ask an adult for help. When your cat hesitates or doesn't want to go, you've gone high enough. Lower it to the level he's comfortable with using.

TEACHING THIS
can be useful when you want to train
your cat to stay off the furniture, too.
Ask your cat to jump when you want
to get her off a surface where she doesn't
belong, like your kitchen counter.
(Review the ways to keep your cat off the
counter on page 136.)

JUMP
From Chair to Chair

This trick is great for acrobatic cats! You've probably seen your pet perform gymnastic-like feats around your home, leaping from surface to surface to get around the room. This trick is a focused version of that behavior.

Your cat will need to have mastered the "Jump" command (page 98) before doing this trick.

INSTRUCTIONS

1. Grab an adult and choose two chairs that are the exact same height. Use regular dining chairs with backs and not stools. If your cat falls while doing the trick, you don't want her to be too high off the ground, because she could get hurt.

2. Put the chairs with their seats facing each other and the bottom edge of each seat touching.

⚠ **SAFETY FIRST**

YOU CAN move the chairs an inch or two (2.5–5 cm) farther apart and use the target to see if your cat will make the jump. If she's hesitant, don't force her! This trick might not be for every cat. Even if she likes it, don't pull the chairs too far apart. If you keep the chairs about one foot (30 cm) apart, this trick will still be impressive.

---

3. Place your cat on one chair. Hold your target on the other chair and tell your cat to jump.

4. Click and reward her if she jumps to the other chair to reach the target. Repeat this at least five times or until she appears comfortable making the leap.

5. Move the chairs apart about two inches (5 cm). Use the target to lure your cat from one chair to the other. Say "Jump" and then click and reward her for her leap.

Expert

Once your cat has mastered the "Jump" command, you can use it to get her to jump on and off items in your home. Practice this with the target first. Get your cat to jump off a table or onto a chair by moving the target around and giving the "Jump" command, followed by a click and a reward. Work up to her jumping to a spot you point to when you give the command. Remember: Never put her on a surface that is too high!

JUMP
Onto Your Knee

Beware of claws! You'll definitely want to wear a pair of thick pants, like corduroys, jeans, or even snow pants, for this trick. Your cat might dig his claws into your leg when he jumps. But the jeans will protect you, and the resulting trick is paw-sitively adorable.

INSTRUCTIONS

1. Place your cat on a chair.
2. Put your foot on the chair with your knee bent, making sure the top part of your leg is parallel with the floor.
3. Hold a treat above your knee. Click and reward your cat when he reaches for the treat with his paw above your knee. Repeat this at least five times.
4. Hold the treat up a little higher. Click and reward him as your cat makes progress moving up your knee. Repeat this at least five times.
5. Get your cat to jump all the way up by withholding the treat unless he is atop your knee. Some cats might not want to do this if the top of your leg doesn't look like a safe landing pad for them. If your cat won't jump onto your knee during the first session, try again at your next one.
6. Once your cat jumps onto your knee, click and reward him. Repeat this five times.
7. After your cat has mastered steps 1 through 6, add a command. Place the treat above your knee and say "Knee." Click and reward him when he jumps. Repeat this trick with the command at least five times.

Cats have **whiskers** on their **front legs.**

DR. GARY'S **VET TIPS**

Here at the San Diego Humane Society, we always want to make sure that animals are treated with kindness and compassion. There is nothing wrong with training animals to perform. In fact, it helps to convince people that they can successfully train their animals, too, and that keeps animals out of shelters. It's important that the owners of a cat circus provide a safe and healthy home for the cats. They should never force the animals to perform and should always use positive reinforcement and not punishment to train them. As long as trainers stick to those guidelines, shows with performing cats can be enjoyable entertainment for everyone involved—including the cats.

Amazing
CIRCUS CATS

When you think of a circus, you may think of clowns and tightrope walkers and daredevils swinging from a trapeze. But have you ever seen a circus with performers that are common house cats?

Trained-cat acts have become increasingly popular in recent years. You can find them all over the world, in places like Russia, Japan, and South Korea—and also in the United States. In some shows, the cats perform with dogs, and at least one show features cats and rats as costars!

All these acts have something in common: They showcase cats performing spectacular tricks. Cats jump through hoops and ride skateboards. They walk on high wires and push barrels. In one act, a cat pushes a mini shopping cart with a dog inside it.

Tricks aren't the only things these shows have in common. Many of these acts adopt rescue cats from animal shelters. Their forever owners work with the cats to find out what their strengths are. A cat that loves to jump will end up jumping through hoops. One that loves to use its paws may end up playing a toy piano.

In all these shows, the trainers know that sometimes the cats won't cooperate. When they don't, the audience seems to like it. After all, one reason people love cats is because of their independence. It's great to see these kitties perform tricks, but it's just as much fun to see them be their true, unique selves by turning up their noses and walking away.

Are you curious to see a cat circus? There may be one coming to town near you. Until then, there are plenty of clips online or on television. In 2018, an act called the Savitsky Cats even made it to the quarter-finals of the TV show *America's Got Talent*.

Siamese cats are likely the most **vocal** breed.

5

PROBLEM-SOLVING

CATS DON'T ALWAYS BEHAVE the way we want them to in a human environment, and sadly many owners get frustrated with their cat's unwanted behaviors. We never want that to happen to you! Luckily, most of the time, there are simple solutions to the problems you're having with your cat. Some unwanted behaviors are caused by health problems that can be fixed. Some can be solved with training. And other problems have less to do with your cat and more to do with how you interact with your kitty and set up your home.

In this chapter, you'll find preventive care and solutions to common behavior problems. Grab an adult and let's give these feline fixes a try.

TOOLS FOR CORRECTIVE TRAINING

You'll need basic training tools for the activities in this chapter, and depending on your cat, you might need some special ones, too:

▶ A cat training clicker (page 34)
▶ A target stick (page 40)
▶ A pheromone-based calming spray (page 53)
▶ Aluminum foil
▶ A citrus-scented spray

Preventive **CARE**

Sometimes, a cat's unwanted behavior can be caused by illness or other health problems. Even before you get to correcting your cat's unwanted behavior, make sure your pet is as healthy as can be. These tips will help you stop problems before they start.

Vaccinate

All cats need to be vaccinated for distemper, the common vaccine name for a group of viruses that cause flu-like symptoms. Depending on their lifestyle, some need other shots, such as rabies. Vaccines are usually given once every three years. Talk to your vet to find out what shots your cat needs and when she needs them.

Feed Them Wet Food

Cats do best with canned food, which is moist, meaning it has water in it. They need lots of water but often don't drink enough on their own. Wet food adds water to their diet and helps prevent health problems.

Let Them Eat Grass

Cats enjoy munching on special varieties of grasses that you can find in a pet store. Eating cat grass may help them process hair balls or even freshen their breath!

Get Them Checked Out

A yearly health exam is important for every cat. Cats who go outside (remember: preferably on a leash) really need to have their poop checked by a doctor. They're at most risk to get parasites—tiny organisms

that steal nutrients from your cat—from the outdoors. Your parents will need to bring a stool sample to your vet once a year, along with your cat!

Remove Fleas

Using a flea comb and with an adult's help, gently comb your cat on the back and down by the tail to look for fleas. If you find any, have your parents ask your veterinarian for a flea preventative for your cat. These are safe medications you apply orally or topically once a month to keep your cat free of fleas year-round.

Keep Teeth Clean

It can be a challenge to learn how to brush your cat's teeth, so ask your vet to show you and your parents how to do this at home using a special toothbrush and paste. Never use your own toothpaste! An adult will need to help you with this one, but with some effort, it can really pay off.

Brush Cats Daily

Brushing helps prevent hair balls and will increase the bond between you and your cat. This is where teaching the "Sit" command can really help!

Help With Hair Balls

Cats get hair balls when hair clumps up in their digestive tract after they groom themselves. There are a few over-the-counter products you can feed to your cat that will help her safely pass the hair balls instead of coughing them up. Ask your vet which one is best for your cat.

Keep Ears Clean

Learning how to clean your cat's ears properly will keep your cat from getting an ear infection or from becoming a home for ear mites, which are a tick-like arachnid. Ask an adult to help you learn.

Decrease Stress

Stress is the cause of most behavior issues with cats. One way to relax your cat and improve her mental health is to play a game that simulates hunting, something she would do in the wild. Playing with cat toys, like stuffed mice, allows cats to explore and be active.

There's No Such Thing as a **BAD CAT**

Imagine that you go to a friend's house. You walk through the front door, and your friend starts yelling at you: "Bad! You're not supposed to wear shoes in the house!"

You'd probably be confused, and maybe even upset. Why is your friend yelling at you and calling you "bad"? If there was a rule about shoes in the house, why didn't he tell you?

This is probably how your cat feels when you call her "bad" for doing something you don't want her to do. For the most part, your cat's behavior stems from her nature. Cats in the wild are born to hunt, protect their territory, and eat. When we invite them into our homes, cats still want to do these same things they would do in nature. But, as you know, these natural behaviors can cause problems in your home. Keep in mind your cat doesn't understand that she's doing something wrong. She's just doing what she was born to do.

None of these things make your cat bad. So before you say "Bad kitty!" take a deep breath and try to figure out what is causing your cat's behavior. Then try to make any adjustments so that she'll stop.

DR. GARY'S **VET TIPS**

Often, there are simple solutions for "bad" cat behaviors. One common unwanted behavior in cats is walking on kitchen counters. A few years ago, I was at a dinner party, and the family cat was walking all over the counters. It is unhealthy to eat food that is prepared on the same surface where a cat has walked, since we all know those paws were recently in the litter box! This problem has some simple solutions. Never place your cat on the counter or feed her there. Use gentle ways to discourage her, such as spraying the counter with a citrus scent. We'll learn more about gentle ways to discourage pets—called negative reinforcement—in this chapter.

The **tufts of fur** on the inside of your **cat's ear** are called **ear furnishings.**

NEVER PUNISH
Your Cat

When your cat develops a behavior that you don't like, there are different ways you can handle it. Positive reinforcement is the best way to teach animals new behavior. An example of positive reinforcement is when you use a click and a treat to get your cat off the table. It's positive because you're not punishing her for being on the table; instead, she's being rewarded for doing the right thing. Positive reinforcement is best for changing behavior and the first thing you should always try.

In rare cases, negative reinforcement is more effective. Negative reinforcement is when you use something your cat doesn't like—such as a touch, taste, or sound—to get him to stop doing something. For example, cats don't like the crinkly sound or cold feel of aluminum foil. If your cat is scratching the leg of a couch, you can cover it with aluminum foil so that he'll stay away from it. That is negative, but it's different from punishing your cat.

Punishing your cat by yelling, hitting, or swatting at him, or harming him in any way, is something you should never, ever do. Besides hurting your cat, these kinds of actions will also stress him out, which may make his bad behavior worse.

In this section, you'll find a mix of positive-reinforcement techniques and some ideas for gentle negative reinforcement. Let's use these to make for a happier cat—and a happier home!

"NO"

We want you to use positive reinforcement to train your cat whenever you can. But there are some situations when a firm "No" can be used to quickly stop your cat from getting into trouble. For example, if he has climbed onto the kitchen counter and is sniffing at dinner bubbling on the stove, say "No" firmly—but do not yell. Pick him up and put him on the floor. Tell him "Sit" then when he does, click and give him a treat. Use the clicker to teach "No," and soon you'll be able to use this cue to get your cat out of sticky situations in a snap.

Loud VOCALIZING

MEEEOOOWWW! Your cat is making a ton of noise, and you're not sure why. Yelling the words "Be quiet!" won't help. So what should you do?

First, remember that most adult cats vocalize, or make noises, only toward humans, not to other cats. They usually make these sounds because they want something.

How can you figure out what they want? Stop what you are doing. Observe your cat and pay close attention to what's happening when he is making a racket. Try to figure out the source of the problem, and then take steps that will quiet him down. Your kitty might be crying for one of these reasons:

Your Cat Is Hungry

Many cats meow when they want to be fed. Feeding them will stop the loud noises, but that only teaches a cat to vocalize when he's hungry. To stop this behavior, teach your cat to sit (page 72), and then have him sit quietly for a few minutes before you feed him. This may teach him that he needs to be quiet before he gets his dinner.

Your Cat Can't Get What He Needs

Is the door leading to the litter box closed? Is his water bowl empty? Give a quick check to make sure he has access to all his basic needs.

Your Cat Wants Attention

Perhaps he needs a good play session to let off some steam. If he wants attention in the middle of the night, ignore him by refusing to let him into your bedroom; or if that's impossible, do not look at him or pet him. When you wake up, be sure to give him lots of attention and playtime. If you can tire out your cat during the day, he will not be as energetic at night.

Your Cat Is Stressed

Your cat might be making noises because he sees a cat outside, or birds in a tree, or a pet near your home that he doesn't like. Help him relax by closing the curtains or putting him in a safe space until the thing that's causing him stress has gone away. For other common reasons that your cat may be anxious, see page 123.

DR. GARY'S **VET TIPS**

Finding the source of what's stressing your cat can be hard, and fixing it can be even harder. If your cat keeps vocalizing no matter what you do to relieve her stress, it's time to call in a cat behaviorist. Animal behaviorists come in many forms. They can be trainers who are certified in cat behavior or vets or scientists who are certified by the Animal Behavior Society. Many vets have experience in behavior even if they're not behaviorists.

BITING and SCRATCHING Humans

Cats bite and scratch their owners for a variety of reasons. They might feel afraid or threatened. Sometimes they use their teeth and claws to play with you. It could be that a cat does not like the way you are petting her or playing with her. Or she might be trying to tell you something, like "Hey, I'm hungry!" No matter what the reason, this is behavior you do not want to encourage. While it's OK for her to play like this with other cats, it can hurt humans. What should you do?

If It Happens While Playing

If your cat gets excited and bites you when you play with her, stop playing with her. Generally, when cats nip, they want us to stop what we're doing to them. Stop and play with her another time.

If It Happens While Petting

If you are petting your cat and she suddenly lashes out at you, perhaps you touched her in a place that makes her uncomfortable. Petting a cat over and over in one place can aggravate her. When this happens, stop. Then spend some time during shorter petting sessions learning how your cat best likes to be handled.

If She's Trying to Get Your Attention

If your cat nips to try to get you to do something, such as feed her, ignore her by turning your back on her and walking away. Follow through with the action (such as feeding her) when she is calm and not biting you.

If You Can't Figure Out Why

Some cats will bite and scratch you no matter what you seem to do. Make sure you've tried to identify everything that could cause your cat stress in her environment, such as loud noises or a lack of a quiet place for your cat to chill out. If you can't find any cause for her stress, talk to your vet about possible causes and solutions for this problem. Sometimes medications are needed to decrease stress in your cat.

CAT TALES

When a sweet white cat named Finn moved into his forever home from an animal rescue group, he was terrified. He hid under a bed and wouldn't come out. Finn's owner spent time lying on the floor with him and playing soothing music. This calmed Finn down, and he finally came out for food and water.

FIGHTING
With Other Cats

If your cat picks fights with other cats he meets in the neighborhood, the solution is very simple: Don't let your cat go outside! If your cat doesn't get along with the other cats in the house, the problem can be a little more complicated to solve. Fortunately, there are some things you can do:

Spay or Neuter

Male cats in particular can become aggressive with each other when they are not neutered. They will be a lot calmer after the procedure.

Give Them Space

The problem might be that your cats are fighting over territory. Make sure that each cat has his own bed, litter box, and food bowl—and that they are all identical, so your cats won't fight over who gets the best one! Adding extra perches to your home, such as cat trees or cat condos, will give cats more places to hang out away from each other.

Reward Good Behavior

When your cats do interact nicely with each other, be sure to give them positive reinforcement, such as treats, praise, or their favorite toys!

Separate Them

Do your cats still not get along? Keep them apart. Close each in their own room with a bed, a litter box, food, and water. If possible, put them in rooms next to each other with their food bowls on either side of the door, so they can eat together without actually being together. After a few days, switch rooms so they get used to each other's scent. Then slowly open the door between them. If they immediately start to fight, shut the door.

Stick With It

If separation isn't working, that means you need to continue to keep them separate for a longer period of time. When more time has passed, get someone to help you reintroduce them for a short period of time once a day. That way, one person can keep an eye on each cat and pull them away if they start to fight. Add a pheromone-based spray diffuser to help them stay calmer. Keep them apart until they show you that they can get along during their supervised play sessions.

What If Nothing Works?

Get help. Bring in a cat behaviorist, who will try to identify the issue and give advice.

DR. GARY'S **VET TIPS**

The more cats you have, the more likely it is that you will have problems between them. I recommend no more than three cats in any household—and two is best.

URINATING OUTSIDE
the Litter Box

If your cat is urinating outside the litter box and onto the floor, then your cat has a litter box problem. If your cat is spraying urine on a vertical surface such as a wall or the side of a couch, that's a slightly different problem (see page 124). Let's start with some solutions to urinating outside the litter box:

Give Him His Own Box

Do you have multiple cats? Make sure each cat has his or her own litter box. Cats don't like to share.

Clean the Litter Box

Is your litter box clean? Cats won't use one if it's full. You should spot-clean the litter box daily and completely change the litter once a week.

Check the Litter Box

What's your litter box setup? Your cat might be avoiding the box if the litter is too deep, or if she doesn't like the feel of the litter, or if she doesn't like the cover (many cats dislike doing their business in a covered box).

Experiment with different setups to find out what she likes.

Observe Your Cat

Is your cat easily able to walk in and out of the litter box? If it looks like she can't step in and out without difficulty, she may have arthritis or another health issue, so she should be seen by a vet.

Watch for Stress

Stress might be causing your cat to urinate outside the litter box. The best thing you can do is to try to find out what is irritating, annoying, or stressing out your cat.

DR. GARY'S **VET TIPS**

Earlier in the book we recommended pheromone-based spray as a solution to help a cat get into a cat carrier. This kind of spray can work in other situations, too. Spray the area outside the litter box to keep your cat calm. This may help her use the litter box instead of the floor.

COMMON CAT **STRESSORS**

Much of unwanted cat behavior is a result of your cat being stressed. We talk about stressed-out cats a lot in this book. Here are some of the most common reasons your feline might be frazzled:

- A new place to live or a new home
- Loud music or other noises, such as yelling or construction noise
- A stray cat outside "taunting" your cat through a window
- Another animal outside, such as bird, squirrel, or another pet
- The addition or loss of a pet or a human in the household (such as a new baby)
- A change in the room, such as rearranged furniture
- Flashing lights
- Another cat in the house bullying your cat
- Too many cats in the house (we recommend no more than three per household)

It's not always easy to determine the cause of stress, but you can try. Keep a journal of when your cat seems most agitated and what is happening at the time. Ask yourself if anything has changed in your home. Take note of what is going on outside. It may require some detective work, but with some observation, you might be able to solve the mystery.

Once you figure out the cause, try to remove the stress. If it's a loud noise, turn down the music. Close the curtains or bring your cat into a different room. If it's something that your cat needs to get used to, like a new home or baby, you could try using a pheromone-based spray in the house to help keep him calm until he accepts the change.

⚠ SAFETY **FIRST**

TALK TO YOUR PARENTS about how and when you should take care of the litter box.

SPRAYING Urine

Does your cat spray on a vertical surface, such as a wall? Does the urine have an extra-strong smell? If so, then your cat is probably urine spraying. Cats do this to mark their territory to keep away individuals—both animal and human—that are threatening them or otherwise stressing them out. They also do this to announce that they are looking for a mate. While the problem is similar to not using the litter box, the solutions are slightly different:

Neuter Your Cat

Male cats spray urine more often than females. Neutering your male cat can help stop this behavior.

DR. GARY'S VET TIPS

Some cats spray urine because they don't have an outlet for their hunting energy. Giving him lots of attention and stimulation is important. Try an interactive toy that releases treats when the cat figures out how to get them. These are a great way for your cat to satisfy his wild urges.

Find the Source

If your cat is spraying because he is stressed about something, try to find the cause of the stress and eliminate it. For some common reasons cats get stressed, see page 123.

Ruin the Spot for Him

If your cat sprays in the same spot, you can try to make that spot unattractive to him. With an adult's help, clean the spot using water and an enzyme-based cleaner, which you can find in pet stores and most supermarkets. Or ask your parent to spray rubbing alcohol on the site and wait 24 hours, keeping your cat away from the spot. Be sure to tell everyone in your home that this spot is off-limits for people and cats! After the spot has been cleaned, cover it with aluminum foil. Get an adult to help you, because it can be tricky to affix the foil to a vertical surface. In doing this, you may need to tape the foil up, which could remove the paint. Once the foil is up, set his food dish close to the spot. Your cat probably won't spray where he eats.

Talk to a Vet

Have your parent talk to a vet. Sometimes, anxiety-reducing medication is the only solution that works for urine-spraying cats.

CAT-PROOF YOUR HOME

Here are some things you can do to make your home a safe haven for your feline friends.

- Cats can choke on yarn, thread, or string, so keep those craft supplies safely put away. Roll up the strings on window shades. Hide or tie up computer cords, which could be dangerous if chewed.

- Always keep the door to your washer and dryer closed, because your cat might crawl in there for a nap on the towels without you knowing it. Keep your toilet and garbage can lids shut, too, to keep your kitty out of trouble.

- Tell your parents to keep poisonous chemicals, such as cleaners, in locked cabinets. Keep medicines in closed and locked cabinets, too.

- Read Dr. Gary's tips about unsafe foods (page 35), and make sure you never leave those foods out where your cat can get them.

- If there are burning candles in the house, make sure somebody is always watching them and they are inaccessible to your cat.

JUMPING FROM
High Places

Cats don't usually jump from very high places—they actually fall! In this case, it's us, the owners, who need to be trained to make our homes safe for our furry friends.

Cats are not afraid of heights, and so they often climb to high places on their own. A cat's natural survival instincts will prevent her from jumping from someplace that is too high. However, just because she got up there easily doesn't mean she can't fall. She might lose her balance or become distracted and slip. If your cat loves to explore the very high shelves or ledges in your house, you can choose to add sticky tape to the edges to keep her away, or use aluminum foil for the same effect. Spraying the area with a scent she doesn't like, such as a citrus spray, might work, too. If you do keep her off high shelves, be sure to give her a perch or shelf at a height you feel comfortable with so that she has a safe place where she can observe her domain.

Even more important than keeping cats off high shelves is keeping them away from open windows. In fact, cats falling out of open windows is such a common problem that vets have a name for it: high-rise syndrome. There is one very easy solution to this problem: Never open your windows unless they are screened and the screens are secure. Tell your other family members not to open windows, and if you must open the window without a screen, keep your cat in a safe place away from it.

AMBUSHING

Cats are natural hunters, so as they grow, they practice hunting skills like stalking and ambushing prey. They are learning how to launch a surprise attack from a hidden place, something they would need to know in the wild. Without prey to hunt, cats may direct these attacks toward their owners. That means they could pounce on you as you're walking down the hall, launch themselves onto your leg with their claws, or jump on you when you settle down onto the sofa. These can all result in injuries and damage to items in your home. There are a few strategies you can use to tame your wild cat:

Play Calmly

One way to stop your cat from aggressive behavior is to never play roughly with your kitty. It may be cute when he jumps on your hand and starts nibbling on it, but if you don't stop him, he'll learn that it's OK to do it and may not outgrow the habit.

Give Your Cat Toys

Make sure your cat has toys that he can use to play out his prey instincts. Mind games, such as treat-dispensing toys, are a great way to enrich your cat's environment. We want him to focus on his toys and not on you.

De-stress Your Cat

It's possible that your cat is stressed, and he is taking it out on you. For some common causes of cat anxiety, see page 123. If you can't determine the cause of stress, talk to your vet or a cat behaviorist.

DR. GARY'S **VET TIPS**

Some cats ambush their owners by blocking their owners' path as they try to move around the home. This is attention-seeking behavior. Spending more time with your cat may help the situation, as well as clicker training. Teach your cat to sit whenever he blocks you, and then reward him when he lets you pass.

Destructive
CHEWING

When cats hunt for food in the wild, they often catch big pieces of food, which they have to break up into pieces in order to chew them. Of course, at your house, when being served regular cat food, they don't need to chew this way. So instead, they chew on items in your home—everything from clothing to wires. Our feline friends can definitely damage our stuff, but even more than that, they can hurt themselves. How do we get kitty to stop chomping?

Try a New Chew

It's OK to chew, just not on your computer cords! Giving your cat something appropriate to chew on, such as a cat toy, cat grass, or even special cat dental treats, will often solve the problem.

Spray

If your cat won't stop chewing on dangerous things, such as electrical cords, a bitter-tasting spray can be used to give the items an unpleasant taste. Talk to your parents and vet to find the best spray to discourage your cat from chewing, and where you can use it.

De-stress Your Cat

Cats that won't stop chewing might be stressed. To learn what might be stressing out your cat, see page 123. If you can't find a reason, take your cat to a vet.

Destructive
SCRATCHING

Cats do a lot of scratching in the wild. As we learned earlier, they scratch on trees to mark their territory and leave their scent behind. They also scratch to sharpen their claws. At your home, with no forest in sight, they could scratch on walls, furniture, and even your clothing, if they like the texture. Try these tactics to save your valuables from your little lion's grip:

Get a Scratching Post

The best thing you can do is give your cat something amazing to scratch. Start with a new scratching post (page 56) and see how she responds. If she doesn't respond, it might be that she doesn't like what it's made of, because cats are very picky about the feel of materials. She might prefer sisal to cardboard, for example. Once you determine your cat's favorite material, put up a few scratching posts in different areas of your home. Try placing some near the objects she normally likes to scratch.

Hide It

If offering scratching posts doesn't work, try hiding or covering up the objects that she most likes to scratch.

Make It Awful

Find a way to make the item undesirable (just to your cat). Put aluminum foil on the arms of your couch or double-sided sticky tape on your curtains, since most cats don't like the way either of these feel on their paws.

Trim Those Nails

With an adult, learn how to clip your cat's nails so she won't need to scratch them herself. Ask your vet to show you and your family how to do this at home.

DR. GARY'S **VET TIPS**

Declawing your cat to solve the scratching problem should never be an option. When you declaw a cat, the last joint in each of her toes is removed. The recovery is extremely painful, and afterward the cat will not be able to perform some natural behaviors, such as flexing the paws. All this can lead to behavior problems, too. In my opinion as a vet, this painful procedure is unthinkable and should never be performed for cosmetic or convenience reasons.

Cat Is
MEAN TO DOG

No matter what you've seen in cartoons and movies, cats and dogs are not natural enemies. Millions of cats and dogs live peacefully together over the world. It's true that they sometimes don't get along, but that's usually because they both want the same things: territory, food, and attention from their owners.

Nevertheless, it's upsetting when you see your cat hissing at or attacking your dog. If that is happening in your home, there are a few things you can do:

Offer a Retreat

Your cat might feel threatened by your dog, which is why she's lashing out. Make sure she has a safe place to retreat to, or escape to, alone in your home. Try a closed room with a cat door that is too small for your dog to fit through.

Give It Time

If you're introducing a new dog into the home, start their interactions slowly and steadily. If your cat is acting aggressively, keep them separated at first. Then, with your dog on a leash, introduce them for short periods of time. Always give them treats at the same time and in the same room—never give your dog a treat without also offering one to your cat, and vice versa.

Use a Calming Spray

A pheromone-based spray can work to calm down cats who are exhibiting aggressive behavior.

Give Them Equal Time

Make sure you give both animals enough attention. If you spend more time with one, the other may get jealous.

IF YOU HAVE BOTH a dog and a cat in your home, they will usually learn to communicate—with noises, with the way they look at each other, and with certain movements. Often, they become best friends.

135

WALKING
on the Counter

You might be the kind of owner who gives your kitty free reign of the house, which means your cat can walk anywhere he pleases. But if you're the kind of owner who hates if your cat jumps up on the counter every time you're preparing food, then there are some things you can do to stop her:

Make the Counter a No-Cat Zone

If you don't want your cat on the counter, then you have to always make it off-limits. Don't feed her on the counter in the morning and then get upset when she jumps up on the counter at lunchtime. You're sending her a mixed signal.

Say No

When your cat jumps up, tell her "No" sternly, and put her back on the floor. Do this each and every time.

Offer a Perch

Cats love high places, and that might be why your cat is on the counter. Make sure she has a perch or two in the house that is just as high as your counter, or higher. A tall cat tree or cat condo works great. Encourage her to use it by adding a comfy bed or some of her favorite toys at the top. If you have clicker-trained your cat, click and reward her every time she uses the perch. This will make the perch more attractive to her than your counter.

Make It Unattractive

Place double-sided tape or special sticky mats, which are sold in pet stores, on the counter. Cats don't like to walk on sticky surfaces, and once they think the counter is that way, they will stay off. Aluminum foil, or strips of aluminum foil tape, can also work the same way, as cats don't like how the foil sounds or feels.

Cats—and their wild relatives—are the only mammals that cannot taste sweet things.

WALKING
on the Computer Keyboard

If you've ever sat down at your computer and seen something like "hxflkjaoifertehrtghencaiwueyte" across the screen, you know what happened: Your cat walked on your keyboard again!

There are a few reasons that cats seem to love being around computers, and it's not because they want to do your homework. Computers can be warm; they are usually sitting on a table or desk, which is up fairly high; and your cat likes being around you. But if you want to protect your equipment (and are not ready to see if your cat will write your essay due on Monday), there are a few things you can try:

Train

Teach your cat how to follow a target (page 40). Any time she gets near your computer, use the target to lure her away from the computer and onto her bed. Click and reward her once she is on the bed so that she knows that the goal is to stay on the bed, not on the keyboard.

Distract

If training doesn't work, see if you can find your cat an attractive replacement. Put a small box or cat bed on your desk next to your computer so that your cat will make herself comfortable there instead of on your equipment. You could also try placing a perch right next to your desk, or splurge for a heated cat bed that replaces the warmth of your hard drive that she craves.

Distract Some More

Place lots of cat toys in the room where you keep your computer.

Cover It

You can purchase a plastic cover that fits over your keyboard. You slip your hands under the cover to type, but your cat can no longer lie on the keys.

Make It Unattractive

Add materials to your computer area that your cat will want to avoid. Put double-sided tape or aluminum foil around the edges of your desk so that she won't climb up. You can also use a citrus-scented spray, which most cats dislike, on the furniture near your computer. But never use this spray directly on electronic equipment.

🐈 CAT **TALES**

Katie Kitty is a tortoiseshell who loves to hang around her owner's computer and sleep on her mini hard drive. Katie has overheated the computer, erased computer files, and pulled out wires while her owner was working. Only after her owner placed a five-foot (1.5-m)-tall cat tree next to the fireplace did Katie leave the computer alone.

STEALING
Your Food

It's dinnertime, and you sit down at the table, hungry for your supper. But there's one problem: Every night, your cat jumps up on the table and starts eating from your plate, as if the food is his and not yours.

It might be cute the first time he does it, but letting your cat share your food is not a habit you want to establish. Cats have very specific dietary needs, so we don't want them filling up on human food, which might not have the nutrients they need. Even if you give your cat just a little bit of your dinner, it could contain additives that cats don't need. Overeating, be it human or cat food, can lead to diseases like diabetes.

DR. GARY'S **VET TIPS**

Cats reach their full growth by about nine months of age. Depending on its breed, your kitten may even be close to his full size by seven months old. After a year, many will continue to grow a bit, but it's at a much slower rate. After two years, the only growth you'll see will be a cat who is getting wider. At each stage of his life, make sure he's eating the proper amount of the right foods.

Luckily, there are a few different ways to approach this problem:

Feed Him First

Just before you sit down to eat, feed your cat in his usual feeding spot. If you are both eating at the same time, he will be less likely to bother you. If he gobbles down his food and still tries to get to your plate, place him in another room.

Teach Him How to Follow a Target

Use your clicker training to teach him how to follow a target (page 40). When he jumps up on the table, use the target to direct him to his own special place in your kitchen. That place could be on the floor or on a stool next to you. Click and reward him when he moves to the stool. You can also teach him to sit (page 72) and to stay (page 74) during your meal.

Talk to a Vet

Make sure there is no medical reason your cat is stealing food from you. Does he always seem to be hungry? It may be that he's not getting the nutrients he needs. Ask your vet to help you figure it out.

UP All Night

When your cat keeps you up all night wanting to play, you might conclude that she's nocturnal—mostly active after dark. But actually, most house cats are not nocturnal. Our feline friends are crepuscular. This means they're most active at dusk and dawn, but happy to be hunting and playing at any time of the day or night.

Keeping your cat outside your bedroom may not help if she's at your door creating a racket and hoping to be allowed in. But there are some things you can do to make your evenings more peaceful:

Feed Her

One reason she might try to wake you up in the middle of the night is that she's hungry. Kittens need food at least twice a day until they're a year old. It's OK to feed an adult cat just once a day as long as she has dry food to snack on during the day. You might want to hold off on canned food until nighttime to fill her up and decrease her cravings while you're sleeping.

Set Up Her Bed

If your cat has never been able to sleep quietly at night, then make sure you have a comfortable sleeping spot for her that is outside your bedroom. If you can, set up the spot a few rooms away (or as far away as possible).

Get Active

Make sure your cat gets plenty of activity during the day. If you're not home, leave her toys to play with or a safe perch with a window view. Play with her at night so she's tuckered out when it's time for bed.

Ignore Her

Whatever you do, don't engage with your cat if she wants something during the night. That will only teach her that if she bugs you, she'll get results. Ignoring her won't be easy, but it's the best thing to do.

Other crepuscular animals include **rabbits, deer, bobcats, bears, and skunks.**

ENRICHMENT AND MORE

TO KEEP CATS HEALTHY, we have to give them fresh water, nourishing food, a safe environment, and basic training. But they also need something else: They need to play with you! Play can ...

▶ Relieve boredom. This is important because bored cats can act out in many unwanted ways.

▶ Help keep your cat at a healthy weight. Overweight cats can get diseases such as arthritis and diabetes.

▶ Release any aggression and make him calmer and even friendlier.

▶ Help give your cat confidence.

▶ Help you forge a bond with your cat.

TOOLS FOR ENRICHMENT

You'll need some basic tools for the activities in this chapter:

▶ A cat training clicker (page 34)

▶ Cat toys (page 146)

▶ Cat treats (page 35)

▶ String

▶ A Hula-Hoop or cat training hoop

You may need additional items for some of the activities in this section. Be sure to look for the "You Need" list before you begin an activity.

Cat **TOYS**

When you go to a pet store, you might be overwhelmed by the selection of cat toys. There are bright ones and feathery ones, squeaky ones and furry ones. How do you know which are best for your feline friend? Here is a quick guide to the types of popular toys you may find in a pet shop. Take a look at the suggestions for simple toys you can make at home, too.

Stuffed Toys

Simple, stuffed toys made for cats are the first type of toy you should introduce to your kitten because they are the safest. Make sure you give your pet a toy specifically made for cats—kids' stuffed animals might have small parts or ribbons that a kitty could chew off and choke on. Always watch your cat the first time she plays with any toy to be sure it's safe.

RULES OF **PLAY**

Never play roughly with your cat by making loud noises, pulling on his tail or paws, or encouraging him to attack, bite, or scratch you. When you do that, you are teaching your cat that those aggressive behaviors are OK with humans, when they are not.

Catnip Toys

Catnip is a dried herb. The scent causes some cats to get excited and happy, and when it's added to toys, it can make your cat eager to play. Not all cats respond to catnip, so try out a simple stuffed toy with your cat first to see how she responds.

Wand Toys

A small stuffed animal or feather dangles from a string on a wand. When you wave it in front of kitty, her predator instincts will take over, and she'll try to catch the "prey." For the best ways to play with this kind of toy, see page 150.

Puzzle and Peek-and-Play Toys

Peek-and-play toys have a base with holes in it. Inside the holes are toys or treats. Puzzle toys go further to encourage your cat to find ways to get at the hidden object. These toys tap into those hunting instincts. In the wild, cats explore small nooks and crevices to find mice and other critters to eat.

Paper Bags

Your cat might enjoy hiding in a plain paper bag or pouncing on it to hear the crinkly sound it makes. You can leave a paper bag out to occupy your cat if she's going to be alone— just make sure the bag is safe by removing any handles.

And remember, never let a cat play with a plastic bag!

Crinkle Toys

Some cats like the sound of crinkled paper or plastic because it reminds them of the sound of other animals moving around in rustling leaves. Try crinkling up a piece of paper and tossing it to your cat. You can also find special crinkle toys in pet stores.

Cardboard Cat Castle

Cats love to hide in boxes. So how about making your kitty a custom castle or a sturdy fort? Any box will work, as long as it's big enough for your cat to fit inside. With an adult's help, cut out doors and windows that your cat can easily walk through. Go ahead and decorate with markers, too! Be sure to avoid adding any decorations or tape to it that your cat might chew on or swallow.

IF YOUR CAT IS A FINICKY EATER, you can also try this test with different types of cat food. Try foods with different ingredients, such as fish or chicken. If your cat doesn't like crunchy foods, he might like something soft or soupy. Perform this experiment over a few days, or with a small amount of each kind of food.

TREAT Test

Do you love pizza and hate lima beans? Like people, cats also have foods they love and foods they won't go near. If you find out what treat your cat loves best, you will have greater success when you train him, because the treat will motivate him to respond. Use this method to test what treat your cat loves the best.

YOU NEED

- At least six different types of cat treats. You may want to ask your vet or pet shop if they can give you samples.

INSTRUCTIONS

1. Break up the treats into dime-size pieces so your cat doesn't get a tummy ache from this test.

2. Start with two different types of treats. Put them side by side, and then introduce your cat to them. See which one your cat eats first. If your cat doesn't go for either of the treats, swap in the next two.

3. Put another one of his favorite treats next to a new type of treat. Does he go for his current favorite or the new kind?

4. Put another treat of the type he has just chosen next to the final contender. Which treat does he choose? That's his favorite!

TROUBLESHOOTING: HE WON'T EAT ANY OF THE TREATS!

If your cat does not respond to any of the treats, try the experiment the next day with four to six different types of treats. If that doesn't work, see if he will respond to small pieces of tuna, turkey, or chicken. If he turns up his nose at all these options, then see our suggestions for other rewards you can use while training (page 35).

HUNTING Games

Letting your cat go outdoors to hunt can be dangerous and unhealthy. You don't want her to pounce on something bigger than she is or to get into a fight with another cat. So, what's the solution? Play hunting games with her indoors! It will be fun for you, and it will help her exercise her natural instincts. All this play could make her calmer and more relaxed.

YOU NEED

- Cat treats (page 35)
- A wand toy (page 146)
- String

Hunt for Treats

Hide some of your cat's favorite treats (dry ones only please, not wet) in places where she likes to hang out, like behind a cushion, tucked into a corner of her cat condo, or sticking out from under her water bowl. At first, she'll think she's finding them randomly, but if you do this repeatedly, she'll learn to hunt for her hidden treats each day.

Playful Prey

When you're using a wand to play with your pet, move the end of the toy in the way a mouse or other critter might run. Try moving it quickly at first so that your cat chases it. Let her get it a few times and then pull it away. At the end of your play session, move it slowly to mimic the way a mouse might get tired after a long chase. At the end of the "hunt," always let her "catch" the prey. Give her a treat so that she feels rewarded and gives you back the wand toy.

Fishing Game

Tie a piece of string to one of your cat's favorite stuffed toys. Dangle the toy over a door or a chair and stay on the other side. Move the string up and down so that your cat has to jump for the toy. Be sure to always let her catch it in the end. Make sure to never let her chew on the string and to keep this toy away from her when you're not supervising. Your cat can choke on string, or if she swallows it, the string can get caught in her intestines.

GET CRAFTY FOR YOUR KITTY

Make a simple stuffed fish toy for your cat! Be sure to ask a grown-up for permission before you choose your sock or use any catnip.

YOU NEED
- One sock
- Polyester stuffing or paper packing material
- Catnip (optional)

INSTRUCTIONS
❶ Start with one small, clean sock. A child's sock or an ankle sock works best; an adult sock or sweat sock will be too big.

❷ Fill the toe with polyester stuffing or paper packing material; if you use paper packing, it will make a crinkly sound when your cat plays with the toy. Leave about four inches (10 cm) unstuffed so that you can make the tail. If you are using catnip, add a pinch to the inside with the stuffing.

❸ Tie a knot where the filling stops, so that the leftover sock sticks out like a tail. (Don't use a string to tie the knot; this could be dangerous to your cat.)

❹ Use permanent marker to add eyes, fins, or other decorations. Ta-da! You've made a fish!

Note: If the knot comes untied, immediately take the toy away from your cat and fix it so your kitty doesn't eat the stuffing.

⚠️ SAFETY **FIRST**

ALWAYS BE mindful of what your cat is able to do and what she enjoys doing. Never, ever, force her to do anything. Make sure it's fun for both of you!

KITTY
Agility Course

On social media you can find all kinds of videos in which cats run through agility courses. They look like acrobats. Well, if you have clicker-trained your cat, and he responds to it, your cat can look this cool, too! It's just a matter of taking what you've learned and putting it all together.

Go back to chapter 4 and, with an adult's help, choose three or four advanced tricks to use in your course. Need some ideas for how to put it all together? Here is one example:

INSTRUCTIONS

1. Start by having your cat crawl through a tunnel (page 96).
2. When he emerges from the tunnel, have him jump over a stick (page 98).
3. Get a friend to hold up a hoop for you and have your cat jump through the hoop (page 100).
4. Then lure him up on a chair and end with a chair-to-chair jump (page 102).

Make sure your cat knows how to do each of these individual tricks before you put them together in an obstacle course. The first time you practice with him, use your clicker to coax him through each trick. You might have to reward him after each step, but with enough practice, he might do it with one reward at the very end.

Perform!

Once you and your cat have your routine perfected, put on a performance for your friends and family. Add a fun backdrop or music to your personal kitty circus.

Q: What do you call a kitty that performs in the circus?
A: An acro-*cat!*

JUMP THROUGH HOOP

TUNNEL

JUMP OVER STICK

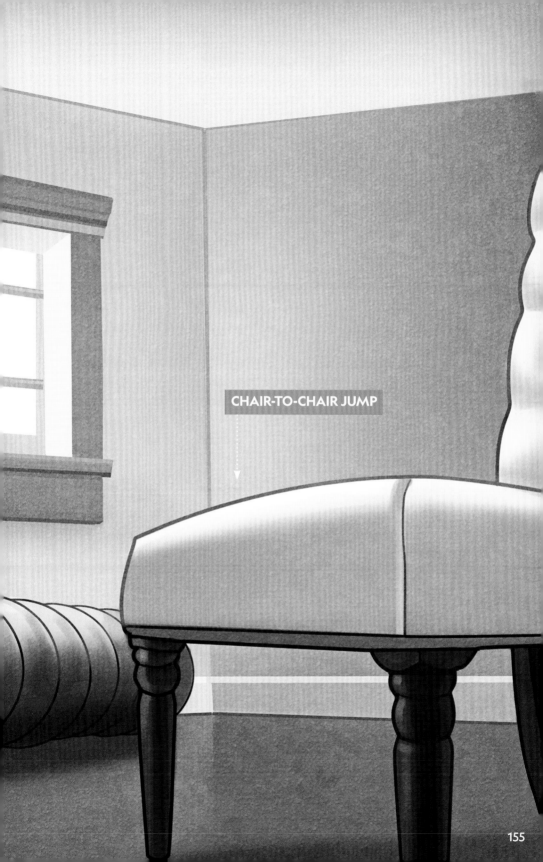

CHAIR-TO-CHAIR JUMP

The Shell **GAME**

This shell guessing game has roots in ancient Greece. "Keep your eye on the ball," a performer tells his audience as he places a ball under one of three identical nutshells. Then he shuffles the shells around quickly. When he stops, he asks the crowd to determine under which shell the ball is hidden.

Sure, this game was devised for humans, but you can play a fun version of it with your cat.

YOU NEED

- Paper cups
- Cat treats (page 35)

INSTRUCTIONS

1. Instead of shells, use two identical paper cups. Sit down on the floor in front of your cat and place the cups in front of her.
2. Take a piece of your cat's favorite treat. Be sure it is small enough to fit under the cup. Let her sniff it.
3. Place the treat under one cup.
4. After you shuffle the cups around without lifting them up, make sure you have your cat's attention.
5. Your cat's curious nature should cause her to knock over the cup with the treat to get it. If she touches the correct cup with her paw, consider that a success!
6. If she chooses the correct cup, she can eat the treat. Pick up the cup to reveal the treat for her if she hasn't knocked it over. If she picks the wrong cup, remove the treat, let her sniff it (but not eat it!), and try again.
7. If your cat masters the game with two cups, make it more challenging by using three cups. You can also use a bell, a ball, or a small toy instead of a treat.

MOST CATS will be interested enough in this game to try to get the treat. If your cat gets up and walks away from the cups, that simply means this trick doesn't interest her. Choose another game for her to play.

Cat CAFÉS

Some people have always wanted to have a cat, but the building they live in, or maybe their parents, won't allow it. In a cat café, you can spend time petting and playing with a cat even if you can't have one at home. Cats live in the café, where they spend their days lounging on cat beds or platforms and soaking up attention. Visitors come to drink a cup of tea or coffee, eat some tasty treats—and, of course, to interact with real cats.

The first cat café opened in 1998 in Asia, and many followed. In Japan, apartment buildings often forbid their residents from owning cats and dogs, which is probably one reason cat cafés became so popular there. In the United States, cat cafés have some particular rules for the health and safety of customers. For example, the cats must stay in a separate area from where food is made, served, and eaten.

Some scientists believe that spending time with a cat can relieve stress and improve your health. Cat cafés can be good for cats, too. In the United States, most cat cafés work with local adoption agencies to match up visitors and cats. Many cats have found forever homes thanks to these cafés.

Of course, if you're already a cat owner, you don't need to go to a cat café for some feline friendship. You could turn your kitchen or living room into your own personal cat restaurant. Ask your family which room is best, then put on some music, grab a beverage, and curl up with your kitty to spend quality time with your favorite feline in your personal cat café.

⚠ SAFETY FIRST

BE CAREFUL with any hot beverages around your cat! Make sure he can't get his paws in it, drink it, or knock it over.

Choose a
CAT NAME

 Congratulations! You've adopted a kitten or gotten a new cat. You're prepared with a litter box, food and water bowls, toys, a scratching post, and a cat carrier. But now you need a name for your pet! Choosing one might be harder than you think. If you're stuck, don't worry. Use some of these ideas for inspiration.

Be Trendy

- Search online for popular cat names, and you'll see some that always pop up.
- Popular female cat names: Nala, Luna, Abby, Bella
- Trendy male cat names: Simba, Milo, Alfie, Binx

Be Colorful

Get inspiration for your cat's name based on his or her color:

- Orange: Ginger, Apricot, Butterscotch, Mango
- Black: Midnight, Ebony, Stormy, Onyx
- Black-and-white: Domino, Checkers, Magic, Sushi
- Brown: Autumn, Chestnut, Fudge, Truffle
- White: Snowball, Tofu, Angel, Creampuff
- Tortoiseshell: Forest, Freckles, Patches, Maze
- Calico: Callie, Amber, Tiger, Caramel

WHAT'S YOUR **CAT'S NAME?**

If your cat already has a name, maybe he needs a nickname, too. Go ahead and use some of these ideas to give him a new nickname.

CAT-NAME GENERATOR

Combine one word from each section to create an unforgettable name for your feline friend.

❶ Month You Were Born

January: Mr./Mrs.
February: King/Queen
March: Lord/Lady
April: Captain
May: Judge
June: Prince/Princess

July: President
August: The Honorable
September: Sir/Dame
October: Brother/Sister
November: Mayor
December: General

❷ First Letter of Your Name

A: Fluffy
B: Silly
C: Happy
D: Bossy
E: Smelly
F: Frisky
G: Sassy
H: Quiet
I: Hissy
J: Cutie
K: Fuzzy
L: Puffy
M: Cranky

N: Cuddly
O: Sweet
P: Funny
Q: Sunny
R: Cheery
S: Testy
T: Perky
U: Jaunty
V: Stinky
W: Sleepy
X: Shiny
Y: Wild
Z: Shy

❸ Your Age

1–5: Feet
6–7: Tail
8–9: Whiskers
10–11: Paws
12–13: Ears
14–15: Fur
16–18: Nose
19–30: Tongue
31+: Ears

Who Is **SMARTER?**

The debate over which adorable pet is smarter has raged between cat and dog owners for years. Who wins? It's complicated.

Cat and dog brains are made up of nerve cells called neurons. These neurons are like little transmitters that send information to different areas of your brain. The more neurons you have, the more capable you are of acquiring knowledge and understanding it.

Dr. Suzana Herculano-Houzel is a neuroscientist who studies animal intelligence by counting neurons in their brains. In 2017, she determined that cats have fewer neurons than dogs. Cats have about 250 million neurons, while dogs have anywhere from 430 million to 620 million. That means dogs have a stronger problem-solving capacity than cats, which explains why they are easier to train.

But wait! That doesn't mean the argument is settled. Neurons are just one way to measure intelligence. Other scientists use observation, interaction, and even brain scans. Also, there are different kinds of intelligence. Dogs might be easier to train, but cats are better hunters—which means they may be better able to survive in the wild. If you look at it that way, what's smarter than knowing how to survive?

The argument will rage on. But really, does it matter? In the end, both cats and dogs give their owners equal amounts of joy.

Cats see things mostly in shades of blue and green.

SACRED Felines

If you think cats are awesome, you have something in common with the people of ancient Egypt.

When family grain supplies started to disappear, the ancient Egyptians discovered mice eating their precious food. Scholars believe that Egyptians realized that cats could help rid their homes of mice and save their grain. The Egyptians started keeping cats as pets and came to believe that these animals were not just useful but were magical—and they brought good luck, too.

Starting about 6,000 years ago, even before Egyptians kept cats as pets, felines were considered sacred. Egyptians worshipped the goddess Bastet, or Bast, who is portrayed as a cat in artworks and known as a protector of women. There were temples dedicated to Bastet, some adorned with her beautiful feline image.

Everyday people and royalty alike kept cats as pets. These furry friends were considered so important that they were preserved to enter into the afterlife with some Egyptian rulers. Thousands of cats were mummified and buried in the rulers' temples and tombs. Mouse mummies have been found along with cat mummies, presumably for cats to snack on in the afterlife!

Of course, you don't have to build a temple for your kitty to show him that you love him. Feed him, play with him, and take him to the vet, and you'll be giving him an honor worthy of ancient Egyptian royalty.

About 1,200 years ago, Vikings took domesticated cats with them on their ocean voyages. These cats helped control rodent populations on their ships.

Your Cat's
SPECIAL STRENGTH

All cats can be trained. But some vets and other cat experts have made observations about cat behavior and identified a few breeds as being better problem solvers, more cooperative, or more eager to learn.

⌣ SIAMESE

These blue-eyed cats with their long, slim bodies like being around people, which makes them more likely to want to be trained. Siamese cat owners report that their cats are good problem solvers that can, for example, figure out how to use door handles to open doors.

⌃ DOMESTIC SHORTHAIR

There might be more domestic shorthair cats in the world than any other breed. These mixed-breed cats are usually very interested in observing their human companions, which makes them good learners. Tabbies, which are shorthair cats with stripes, may be a bit easier to train than other cats because of their relaxed nature and desire to bond.

⇄ SCOTTISH FOLD

Some experts say that they are fast learners, and these cats have a sweet temperament as a bonus.

⟨⇄ ABYSSINIAN

With its long legs, this cat is noted for being athletic and energetic. Some cat enthusiasts think they are the best at completing agility courses. Experts say that this breed has an excellent memory as well.

⟨⇄ SAVANNAH

Veterinarian Dr. Marty Becker says that Savannahs love new challenges, which makes them respond well to training activities.

If your cat isn't one of these breeds, don't worry. Every cat has his or her own special strengths. And just because your cat is on the list doesn't necessarily mean that he or she will be easy to train. Remember, every cat is different!

What KIND of Cat Are You?

If you were a cat, which breed might you be? Take this quiz to find out how your human personality would translate into a feline one. Record your answers on a separate piece of paper.

1. WHAT IS YOUR FAVORITE CLASS OR ACTIVITY?

a. geography
b. gym
c. chorus
d. homeroom
e. free time

2. WHAT'S YOUR FAVORITE THING TO DO OUTDOORS?

a. hiking
b. rock climbing
c. playing volleyball
d. going to the park
e. chilling out by the pool

3. PICK A HOBBY:

a. traveling
b. soccer
c. reading
d. gymnastics
e. napping

4. WHAT IS YOUR BEST QUALITY?

a. I can adapt to any situation.
b. I am very athletic.
c. I get good grades.
d. I am charming.
e. I don't let things bother me.

5. AT A PARTY, YOU ...

a. tell everyone stories of your travels.
b. start a game of basketball in the driveway.
c. entertain everyone by singing.
d. talk to everybody in the room.
e. chill out on the couch.

ABYSSINIAN

BURMESE

RAGDOLL

6. HOW DO YOU FEEL ABOUT DOGS?

a. I think we have a lot in common.
b. Meh. They don't bother me.
c. They're fine, as long as they don't hog up too much attention.
d. They are good companions.
e. I love to cuddle up with them.

7. WHAT'S YOUR FAVORITE COLOR?

a. green
b. red
c. blue
d. orange
e. pink

8. PICK A WEATHER FORECAST:

a. cold and snowy
b. chilly and bright
c. cloudy and cool
d. hot and sunny
e. rainy

SIAMESE

MAINE COON

If you picked mostly a's, you're a ... MAINE COON CAT.

This muscular cat is known for its long, beautiful coat. They are thought to be as friendly and trainable as dogs and make good travelers.

If you picked mostly b's, you're an ... ABYSSINIAN.

With a history going back to ancient Egypt, these active cats love to jump, climb, and explore.

If you picked mostly c's, you're a ... SIAMESE CAT.

These cats are famous for their complex personalities. They're curious and smart and vocalize loudly and often.

If you picked mostly d's, you're a ... BURMESE CAT.

With roots in Thailand and Burma, this breed was developed in Britain and the United States. They are beautiful, charming, and acrobatic.

If you picked mostly e's, you're a ... RAGDOLL CAT.

They are as relaxed and laid-back as the dolls they are named after. They love the cozy feeling of being at home.

Test Your **CAT IQ**

Now that you've worked with your cat to learn tricks from this book, your favorite pet might be jumping through hoops and crawling through tunnels. But did you realize that you've learned something, too? Take this quiz to find out if you're a master of *Pounce!* purr-fection.

1. Humans domesticated cats long before they began keeping dogs as pets. True or False?
2. Why do cats have tails?
   a. to swat at predators
   b. to help them balance
   c. to attract mates
   d. to keep away bugs
3. When are cats best able to learn how to socialize with other animals and humans?
   a. when they are 8 years old
   b. between 8 and 15 weeks old
   c. between birth and 8 weeks old
   d. after their first birthday
4. An adult cat has a shorter attention span than a kitten. True or False?
5. What does it mean when your cat's whiskers point backward?
   a. She is scared.
   b. She is cold.
   c. She is happy.
   d. She has to sneeze.

6. Why do cats like to climb into cardboard boxes?
   a. They like how cardboard feels.
   b. They are marking their territory.
   c. They are drawn to cube-shaped things.
   d. It makes them feel like they are in a safe place to observe their surroundings.
7. Food is always the best reward when training a cat. True or False?
8. About how long should each training session with your cat last?
   a. 20 minutes
   b. 30 minutes
   c. 60 minutes
   d. 10 minutes or until your cat loses interest.
9. Cats and dogs can't learn the same tricks. True or False?
10. Why is it a good idea to keep cats indoors?
    a. It protects them from wild animals.
    b. It protects them from disease.
    c. It protects them from cars.
    d. All of the above.

1. False. Humans started training dogs about 12,000 years before they invited cats into their homes. 2. b. 3. c. 4. False. 5. a. 6. d. 7. False. Food is a good reward for most cats, but some cats prefer toys or praise. 8. d. Don't force your cat to train if she is not in the mood. 9. False. Cats can learn many of the same tricks dogs can, such as sit, stay, and fetch. 10. d.

RESOURCES &
Further Reading

Professional Help

American Society for the Prevention of Cruelty to Animals (ASPCA)

This is America's first animal anticruelty organization. Its website provides information on cat care, nutrition, training, and dealing with behavior issues.

aspca.org/pet-care/cat-care

Humane Society of the United States (HSUS)

This national organization provides direct care to animals through training, sanctuaries, veterinary programs, and animal emergency response.

humanesociety.org/animals/cats

Petfinder

This site links to nearly 11,000 animal shelters all across the United States, Canada, and Mexico. It matches homeless cats (and other pets) with new owners. It also offers cool videos and pet care tips.

petfinder.com

San Diego Humane Society

This organization has been around since 1880 and is one of the largest animal shelters in the United States. Veterinarians learn to treat thousands of animals, animal cops investigate cruelty cases, and professional animal trainers rehabilitate animals with behavior issues.

sdhumane.org

On-Screen and in Print

BOOKS

Cat Breed Guide: A Complete Reference to Your Purr-fect Best Friend
Stephanie Warren Drimmer and Gary Weitzman, D.V.M., National Geographic Kids Books, 2019

Clicker Training for Cats
Karen Pryor, Karen Pryor Clicker Training/Sunshine Books, 2003

How to Speak Cat: A Guide to Decoding Cat Language
Aline Alexander Newman and Gary Weitzman, D.V.M., National Geographic Kids Books, 2015

*National Geographic
Cats Sticker Activity Book*
National Geographic Kids Books, 2017

*National Geographic Kids Readers:
Cats (Level 1 Co-reader)*
Joan Marie Galat, National
Geographic Kids Books, 2017

*National Geographic Kids Readers:
Cats vs. Dogs (Level 3)*
Elizabeth Carney, National
Geographic Kids Books, 2011

*Think Like a Cat: How to Raise a
Well-Adjusted Cat—Not a Sour Puss*
Pam Johnson-Bennett, Penguin, 2011

WEBSITES

National Geographic

"Cats Domesticated Themselves,
Ancient D-NA Shows," Casey Smith
**news.nationalgeographic.com/
2017/06/domesticated-cats-dna
-genetics-pets-science**

"Domestic Cat"
**nationalgeographic.com/
animals/mammals/d/domestic-cat**

National Geographic Kids

Cats Quiz Whiz: **natgeokids.com/
games/quizzes/cats-quiz-whiz**

Cats Rule in Ancient Egypt:
**natgeokids.com/explore/
cats-rule-in-ancient-egypt**

Moment of Meow: **natgeokids.com/
explore/moment-of-galleries/
moment-of-meow**

Animal Planet

"5 Tips to Make Vet
Visits Less Stressful
for Your Cat":
animalplanet.com/pets/
less-stressful-vet-visits/

**Humane Society of the
United States**

"Trimming a Cat's Claws":
humanesociety.org/resources/
trimming-cats-claws

INDEX

PHOTO CREDITS

AS=Adobe Stock; AL=Alamy Stock Photo; GI=Getty Images; IS=iStockphoto; SS=Shutterstock

Cover: front cover (UP), Tony Campbell/SS; front cover (LO), Lubava/SS; spine, Geoffrey Jones/SS; back cover (UP), seregraff/AS; back cover (LO), Antagain/IS; **Introduction:** 2-3, Andrey Kuzmin/AL; 4, Eric Isselée/AS; 5, Ermolaev Alexandr/AS; 6, Christina Hall/San Diego Humane Society; 7, Tony Campbell/AS; 8, Lux Blue/SS; 9, Mint Images RF/GI; 10, ablokhin/AS; 11, Matt Carr/Photodisc/GI; 12-13, Chris Winson/Moment RF/GI; 15, Hayne Palmour IV/San Diego Union-Tribune/ZUMA Wire; 16, Oksana Kuzmina/AS; 17, borchee/IS/GI; 18 (UP), Diederik Hoppenbrouwers/EyeEm/GI; 18 (LO LE), Life On White/Photographer's Choice/GI/GI; 18 (LO RT), imagenavi/GI; 19 (UP LE), taraminchin/IS/GI; 19 (UP RT), elenaleonova/E+/GI; 19 (CTR), BruceBlock/IS/GI; 19 (LO), Kimberlee Reimer/Moment/GI; **Chapter 1:** 20-21, victoriyasmail/AS; 22, Geoffrey Jones/SS; 23, Zoonar GmbH/AL; 24 (UP LE), Shinya Sasaki/MottoPet/Ardea; 24 (UP RT), Daniel Grill/Tetra images RF/GI; 24 (LO LE), janifest/AS; 25 (UP), TungCheung/SS; 25 (CTR), Seregraff/SS; 25 (LO), Cherry-Merry/SS; 26 (UP), Akimasa Harada/Moment/GI; 26 (LO), Sergio Castelli/Dreamstime; 27, Dixi/AS; 28, John Daniels/Ardea; 29, Chris Winson/Moment RF/GI; 30, Anastasiia Skorobogatova/SS; 32, MVolodymyr/SS; 33, Beholder/AS; 34 (RT), Ermolaev Alexandr/AS; 34 (LE), Ermolaev Alexander/SS; 35, Farlap/AS; 37, GoodLifeStudio/IS/GI; 38, Tierfotoagentur/AL; 39 (LE), Grigorita Ko/AS; 39 (RT), bmf-foto.de/SS; 40, Tierfotoagentur/AL; 41, Tierfotoagentur/AL; **Chapter 2:** 42-43, Nils Jacobi/SS; 45, Vergani Fotografia/AS; 46, absolutimages/SS; 47, Andrey Kuzmin/AS; 48, Naenaejung/IS/GI; 49, MoniqueRodriguez/IS/GI; 50-51, Matthew Rakola/NGP; 53, Foonia/SS; 54, Chamrasamee/SS; 55, Yevheniia/AS; 56, cieycbw/Stockimo/AL; 57, kali9/E+/GI; 58, Benjamin Simeneta/AS; 59, NataVilman/SS; 60, Viorika/IS/GI; 61, Eric Isselee/SS; 63 (UP), Warner Bros./Photofest; 63 (LO LE), Everett Collection, Inc.; 63 (LO RT), Bettmann/GI; 64, 101cats/IS/GI; **Chapter 3:** 66-67, M. Watson/Ardea; 68, sanyanwuji/AS; 69, Albina Light/SS; 70, Vera Kuttelvaserova/AS; 71, Frédéric Sécher/EyeEm/GI; 72, Tsekhmister/SS; 73, ArtMarie/E+/GI; 74, PHOTOCREO Michal Bednarek/SS; 75, Westend61/GI; 76, Shinya Sasaki/MottoPet/amana images/GI; 77, Shinya Sasaki/MottoPet/amana images RM/GI; 78, Kin Ming Ho/Moment/GI; 79, Tony Campbell/SS; 80, cynoclub/SS; 81, Juniors Bildarchiv GmbH/AL; 82, pimmimemom/AS; 83, Matthew Rakola/NGP; 84, Bruce Glikas/FilmMagic/GI; **Chapter 4:** 86-87, Tierfotoagentur/AL; 88, Gandee Vasan/The Image Bank/GI; 89, Markus Gauß/EyeEm/GI; 90, Tierfotoagentur/AL; 92, Danny Smythe/SS; 93, Nynke/AS; 94, Jim Madsen; 96, DoraZett/AS; 97, SJ Allen/SS; 98, Akimasa Harada/Moment/GI; 101, Juniors Bildarchiv GmbH/AL; 102, John Daniels/Ardea; 103, Mark Taylor/Nature Picture Library/AL; 105, Jim Madsen; 106, Yuri Kadobnov/AFP/GI; **Chapter 5:** 108-109, tiplyashina/AS; 110, AllaSaa/SS; 111 (UP), FrankvandenBergh/E+/GI; 111 (LO), Lapina/SS; 112, Kachalkina Veronika/SS; 114, Toncha/AS; 115, vdovin/AS; 116, Ekaterina Kolomeets/AS; 117, Yulia_Bogomolova/SS; 118, Diana Taliun/AS; 121, AltamashUrooj/SS; 122, Africa Studio/AS; 123, Marc Henrie/Dorling Kindersley/GI; 125, Africa Studio/AS; 126, Grigorita Ko/SS; 127, oxygen/Moment/GI; 129, Akimasa Harada/Moment/GI; 130, Alexandra Steedman/Image Source/GI; 131, Ronnachai Palas/EyeEm/GI; 132, Paul Kuroda/SS; 134, Jagodka/SS; 135 (UP), Chelsea Victoria/EyeEm/GI; 135 (LO), chendongshan/AS; 136, benevolente/AS; 139, claudiaveja/AS; 140, Juniors Bildarchiv GmbH/AL; 143, Sompop Kongsakul/EyeEm/GI;- **Chapter 6:** 144-145, Alena Ozerova/AS; 146, New Africa/AS; 147 (UP), Kathrin Richter/FOAP/GI; 147 (LO), Saskia Wagenaar/SS; 148 (LO), Grigorita Ko/AS; 148 (yellow rectangle treat), Aleksey Patsyuk/SS; 148 (yellow fish treat), pamela_d_mcadams/AS; 148 (red fish treat), pamela_d_mcadams/AS; 148 (brown rectangle treat), pamela_d_mcadams/AS; 148 (star treat), Aleksey Patsyuk/SS; 148 (yellow oblong treat), Aleksey Patsyuk/SS; 148 (plates), kyoshino/E+/GI; 149, George Rudy/SS; 150, dule964/AS; 151, Matthew Rakola/NGP; 152, GK Hart/Vikki Hart/TaxiGI; 153, Elena Butinova/SS; 154-155, Jim Madsen; 156, Will Heap/DK Images; 157, Juniors Bildarchiv GmbH/AL; 158 (UP), The Asahi Shimbun/GI; 158 (LO), Sergei Konkov/TASS/GI; 159, Lise Gagne/IS; 160, Idamini/AL; 161, kuban_girl/AS; 162, Grigorita Ko/AS; 163, jagodka/AS; 164, Metropolitan Museum of Art; 165, AmandaLewis/IS/GI; 166 (UP), Axel Bueckert/AS; 166 (LO), Vladyslav Starozhylov/SS; 167 (UP), Vladyslav Starozhylov/SS; 167 (CTR), nelik/SS; 167 (LO), Eric Isselee/AS; 168 (Abyssinian), cynoclub/IS/GI; 168 (Burmese), Marc Henrie/Dorling Kindersley/GI; 168 (ragdoll), Erik Lam/SS; 169 (Siamese), Jagodka/SS; 169 (Maine coon), Ivanova N/SS; 171, David Shopper/Corbis/GI; 172 (UP), fantom_rd/SS; 172 (LO), nvelichko/AS; 173 (UP), Maxim Slesarchuk/AS; 173 (LO), Oksana Kuzmina/AL

For all the incredible heroes working in kitten nurseries to save the babies!
—Dr. Gary Weitzman

Since 1888, the National Geographic Society has funded more than 12,000 research, exploration, and preservation projects around the world. The Society receives funds from National Geographic Partners, LLC, funded in part by your purchase. A portion of the proceeds from this book supports this vital work. To learn more, visit natgeo.com/info.

NATIONAL GEOGRAPHIC and Yellow Border Design are trademarks of the National Geographic Society, used under license.

For more information, visit nationalgeographic.com, call 1-877-873-6846, or write to the following address:

National Geographic Partners
1145 17th Street N.W.
Washington, D.C. 20036-4688 U.S.A.

Visit us online at nationalgeographic.com/books

For librarians and teachers: nationalgeographic.com/books/librarians-and-educators

More for kids from National Geographic: natgeokids.com

National Geographic Kids magazine inspires children to explore their world with fun yet educational articles on animals, science, nature, and more. Using fresh storytelling and amazing photography, *Nat Geo Kids* shows kids ages 6 to 14 the fascinating truth about the world—and why they should care. **kids.nationalgeographic.com/subscribe**

For rights or permissions inquiries, please contact National Geographic Books Subsidiary Rights: bookrights@natgeo.com

Designed by Angela Terry

National Geographic supports K–12 educators with ELA Common Core Resources. Visit natgeoed.org/commoncore for more information.

Library of Congress Cataloging-in-Publication Data

Names: West, Tracey, 1965- author. | Weitzman, Gary, author.
Title: Pounce! how to speak cat training guide / by Tracey West & Gary Weitzman, D.V.M., President & CEO of the San Diego Humane Society.
Description: Washington, DC : National Geographic Kids, [2020] | Includes index. | Includes bibliographical references and index. | Audience: Ages 8-12 | Audience: Grades 4-6 | Summary: "Guide to training a cat for kids, based on scientific information about felines"-- Provided by publisher.
Identifiers: LCCN 2019035910 | ISBN 9781426338465 (paperback) | ISBN 9781426338472 (library binding)
Subjects: LCSH: Cats--Training--Juvenile literature.
Classification: LCC SF446.6 .W47 2020 | DDC 636.8/0887--dc23
LC record available at https://lccn.loc.gov/2019035910

The authors and book team would like to thank the following individuals: Amanda Kowalski, MS, CPDT-KA, director, San Diego Humane Society Behavior Center; Jackie Noble, manager, San Diego Humane Society Kitten Nursery. The publisher would like to thank everyone who worked to make this book come together: Erica Green, project manager; Angela Modany, associate editor; Lori Epstein, photo director; Nicole DiMella, photo editor; Brett Challos, art director; Callie Broaddus, senior designer; Robin Palmer, fact-checker; Alix Inchausti, production editor; and Anne LeongSon and Gus Tello, design production assistants.

Printed in China
20/RRDH/1